Love Notes from the Soul:

STORIES OF TRANSFORMATION & HOPE

EDITED BY
CYNTHIA GREGORY

Mayacamas Press
Sonoma, California

ISBN Registration
Tradepaper: 978-1-7375749-3-4
eBook: 978-1-7375749-4-1

Edited by Nora Joanne Gerber
Cover design by Mariah Miller
Interior layout by Crissi Langwell

Printed in the United States of America

FOREWORD

In early 2023, I was invited to celebrate the eightieth birthday of a dear friend along with a small tribe of fellow seekers on a silent retreat. Following a serpentine drive down US Highway 1, we landed at a spectacularly beautiful monastery perched high above California's pristine Pacific coast. I don't know what wisdom I was expecting –or hoping– would drop in my lap during those three days of contemplation and journaling, meditating to the chanting of the monks, or sitting outdoors where a light fog gently kisses a hillside that drops away into the sea below…but it wasn't a book. Certainly, not something as certifiably *woo* as a book called *LOVE NOTES From the Soul.*

But there I was, reading Mary Oliver, getting cracked open by images of her rural New England, sitting lotus style on a bench built into the cliffs above Big Sur. In that soft sunlight, I received the seed of an idea that somehow germinated before blooming into something bigger. The blossoming required trust, and a shock sure faith in the big idea. Throughout this endeavor, I maintained an absolute belief in the idea; but trust required practice. One of the greatest learnings I garnered in the process of co-creating this book is that when fate conspires with destiny, miracles happen. And it turns out that just as I warmed to the idea of collecting and publishing stories of hope by genius authors, our beautiful planet and perhaps civilization itself was, as Yeats coined the phrase, "Slouching Towards Bethlehem."

Sometimes the idea for a book comes as a single thought. Sometimes a book is born from the warm remains of a sentence spoken in passing. Sometimes, a book comes to you fully formed and wrapped in a bow –albeit with an essential piece missing. That is how LOVE NOTES was born; fully formed and with a piece missing. The vital piece absent was what would become the tribe of contributing writers whose combined wisdom made a genius book that is greater than the sum of its parts.

As a writer, I have always been fascinated by story. Growing up, my sister and I shared a pink bedroom with cabbage-rose pattern curtains where we would tell each other stories at night when we couldn't sleep. Those stories shared in the dark all those years ago formed a bedrock. Years later when my sister moved from the wilds of Washington state to the vast, undulating plains of the Midwest, I flew from Los Angeles to Seattle and we drove together across the Columbia River Basin, through Spokane, traversed the panhandle of Idaho, crossed Montana and North Dakota, before dipping into Minnesota. During this sisterly sojourn, one of the passenger's jobs was to read aloud, *The Lone Ranger and Tonto Fistfight in Heaven,* by Sherman Alexie. We surfed Alexie stories across fertile river valleys, through forests and bisecting plains, compelled by the ancient art of the well-crafted narrative.

Stories feed us. They instruct and in the best cases, elevate our souls. They show us who we are and who we endeavor to be. When the stories of LOVE NOTES began to arrive, they did so like the first snow in winter. Slowly, softly, little miracle stories began to float and flurry and soon created a gravitational pull of their own, attracting ever more stories. I fell in love repeatedly as I read these author's expressions of quiet courage, fierce love, and an unapologetic thirst for meaning.

The thirty voices representing this community of writers are nothing short of miraculous. The vision was always to provide a place for relentlessly authentic new voices to be seen and heard, and to elevate ideas that represent the best of the human spirit. These are a small offering of the thousand invisible stories of everyday heroes, of mothers and fathers, sons and daughters, lovers, teachers, artists, healers, and ancestors.

All on their own, the stories arrived, stacking up, forming drifts, exposing intersections of theme and content across the complete work. I found threads connecting ideas between stories, I found certain universal truths appearing again and again: Pause. Practice gratitude. Notice what lives in the liminal spaces. Love everyone you can. Forgive yourself. In these stories, in these sacred spaces, the human experience rises like something holy. I know that I have learned to trust the process of crafting a powerful story, a transcendent story, and am, and will forever more be, deeply gratified to curate this artful, magical compilation.

Cynthia Gregory
Editor and Curator

Table of Contents

1

LOVE IN THE THIRD ACT

Kelly Mason

Fade in: A woman of a certain age stands at the pinnacle of a rocky outcrop. Below her, the whole world.

Many stories are told in a three-act structure. The first act is the setup and establishes the character arc, the second act opens with the central conflict and the rising action that will fundamentally change the main character for better or worse, and the third act is the final resolution, the ending. A significant third act includes a denouement illuminating the rest of the plot, tying all the loose ends together, and making sense of all that has gone before.

For a third-act turning point to be meaningful, the protagonist must embrace the ultimate truth. What are the risks, what must be overcome, and what is at stake? They become selective about what experiences to include and intentional about what to set aside. There will be challenges that appear insurmountable. It's a low point and they're feeling defeated, ready to give up, and telling themselves that to do so would be fine.

A big turkey buzzard smacked headlong into my car windshield. Scavenging for roadkill, it was just lifting off as my car rounded the bend. First, there was a sickening thump. I lost sight of the road in a mass of black feathers. "You did that to yourself," I shouted, sorrowful at the thought of killing any living thing, even a buzzard. My heart pounding, I continued down the mountain.

Folklore tells us that a bird represents transition. As it turns out, a bird hitting your window is synonymous with one door closing and another opening. I read that it could mean the end of a relationship that's no longer working for you or quitting a job that's distressing you. That was one big bird, I thought, so buckle up! Scrolling through the top articles on birds hitting a windshield, of which there are many oddly enough, I filtered my search with a new criterion. What is the spiritual significance of a bird hitting the windshield? I hit enter and the Universe responded … Sankofa.

Sankofa is a word from the people of Ghana that means "to return and retrieve it." It refers to the Bono Adinkra symbol represented by a stylized heart shape or by a bird with its head turned backward while its feet face forward. The bird carries a precious egg in its mouth. The spirit of Sankofa urges one to take what is good in the past and bring it into the present moment to create a brighter future. A well-told story does the same.

My third act begins with an ending, which is not unusual. My classroom watched with fascination as our caterpillars metamorphosed into butterflies. On the last day of school, a release ceremony was held. It was a wondrous day. At first, our butterflies didn't fly away, instead landing on the back of our hands. One even landed on a child's head. The release ceremony held greater meaning for me because the children and I were saying goodbye. It was one of the most memorable lessons I've ever taught.

I was employed by a company that can only be described as having a toxic workplace. Nobody worked there long, and morale was low. In retrospect, I don't know how I managed to remain as long as I did. My last day was triggered by my supervisor chastising me for allowing the children to go outside and release their butterflies. When I received censure for holding the release ceremony, I knew I had to resign. Five Painted Ladies got their wings that day, six if you count me!

It's a bold move to quit a job without an offer on the table. I didn't know what I would do, I only knew I wouldn't do that anymore. The people in my corner, the people who love me, applauded, but it was risky. There was a lot at stake.

Poignancy is elemental to a great third act and it's the same with the experience of Sankofa, which honors our personal struggle to become who we are. Why would I carry forward anything from the past that might prevent me from being happy in the future?

People do. If we've lived at all, we do. Yet, something was shifting. I was coming unstuck, could almost feel myself rising. I found myself without an income but instead of being worried, I felt exhilarated. I needed a job. I could go back into the classroom, but did I want to? No. I needed freedom. Embarking on a writing career in my forties, I had achieved a measure of success, but I'd shelved all that to teach full-time. And so, I determined to reclaim that part of myself and take it into the future. How did I know that Sankofa wasn't done with me yet?

The next seismic shift in my third-act resolution is not something I can be simplistic about. My living arrangement with a former partner was that of a loving friendship and had been for many years. Our arrangement was a mutually beneficial albeit lonely way to live. I told myself it was good enough, mature even. We had great conversations, shared a love of playing music, and knew all the same people. It was a compromise, but in retrospect, not a good one. It was dishonest and disingenuous to say that I didn't want and need to be seen, to give and receive affection, to be loved.

What is the call to action? How will your character arc resolve? What is the essential truth waiting to be uncovered? If you'd been following along as this story unfolded, you'd know that an interesting subplot was in development. Out of the blue, but not really, the setup was nothing short of exquisite, a love interest appeared on the horizon. It's beyond satisfying when a character is blindsided by love.

For over a decade, I'd maintained a friendship with a writer I admired from an online writing group. If it's true that imitation is the sincerest form of flattery, I think I wanted to be him. He's funny, so easy to talk to, and an amazing storyteller. No wonder we were friends, he has many. I say we knew each other but the truth is we had never met in person. Now, this third act turning point brought us to the same city at the same time.

I thought I was too cool and sophisticated to ever be swept off my feet. I was not. How can I explain what it's like to experience the arousal of quiescent forces like love and desire? It takes self-awareness and a measure of grace to find your bearings when you feel familiar ground shifting under your feet.

Finding love in the third act is unlike any love that has come before. At this stage of life, romantic love is tempered, seasoned with wisdom garnered from all that has gone before. I'm comfortable sharing my feelings, expressing my opinion, and giving and receiving support. I know my worth and have no qualms about being myself in a relationship. I can love you and not lose myself in the bargain. It's that simple and that profound. Love wins.

It's my life story. If anyone had told me six months ago that I'd be doing what I'm doing, I'd have laughed and written them off as crazy. I came to Texas in August, despite record-high temperatures and drought conditions, to spend time with a man I had known forever and had only just met. I mentioned to him that we could watch the Perseid meteor shower, something he had never done and something I had only done alone. As I watched him set his alarm for three fifteen, prime time for a meteor shower, I felt a certainty in my heart, unlike any time before, that here with him was where I have always belonged.

Meteors are part of the tail of a comet and the ones we would see come from the direction of the constellation Perseus, the legendary son of Zeus and the slayer of the Gorgon Medusa. In this compelling hero's journey, Perseus completes his quest against all odds. On his way back, he sees a beautiful woman chained to a rock. She's about to be eaten by a giant sea monster. Perseus falls in love with Andromeda and saves her from sacrificing her own life in service to others. In the third act of the Perseus myth, the couple marry and live a long life together.

I've lived long enough to understand that nothing is promised. Knowing that only fuels my desire to live better, experience more, and love deeply. Those of you in the process of writing your own third act, ask yourself what you'll take with you and what you will set aside. Make choices that reflect your innermost desires and greatest aspirations. Remember that fortune favors the bold. How are you going to conclude this great work of art, your phenomenal life story?

I was fast asleep and dreaming when the alarm went off. I woke with a start, feeling a bit disoriented, unsure of where I was until I heard him say it was time to go. He was already dressed and had a blanket under his arm. I said, "Oh boy, oh boy," something we still laugh about, throwing on my clothes in a rush. I was carried away by the anticipation of watching shooting stars with this man who loved me and making wishes that might even come true. At a nearby park, we spread out our blanket on the ground. Holding hands and lying on our backs, we counted all the meteors we saw, pointing them out to each other as we watched them streak across the night sky.

2
THE MOST POPULAR GIRL IN THE ICU

Erin Partridge

I am on the cusp of a new beginning in my life and my career. I am an artist, art therapist, researcher, and professor. I am also an advocate for aging with curiosity and creativity. The path to where I stand today took strange turns over the past few years. During the pandemic, I navigated two near-death experiences and multiple hospitalizations. Though I wish I did not have to endure these scary events, I am stronger for it.

My strength comes with two lessons on the topics of how to be the most popular person in the ICU and how to be the least popular person in the ICU. Both stories contain truths about how we narrate our lives—the way we describe what happens to us and the way we make meaning of it all.

I know that at one point, I was the least popular person in the ICU. But I do not know why. I have a clear memory of standing, disheveled in two layers of hospital gown, nonslip socks, and a fall-risk bracelet on a spindly arm. I stood in the doorway of my shared room in the ICU, holding up a small note I created. "Goal for the day: Do not make any nurses cry." This goal was my contribution to the assigned goals on my patient information board about being oriented to time and place and walking with assistance around the floor.

I do not know what precipitated this goal. I do not remember making any nurses cry, but I do know that I was apparently not a very nice, compliant patient while on steroids to reduce brain swelling. I was in the ICU after having an adverse reaction to a medication during a procedure. I had hundreds of seizures and at least one unwitnessed fall leading to encephalitis and four spinal fractures. I spent time in the emergency, ICU, acute medical, and telemetry floors under the care of hematology, gastroenterology, and neurology. I remember some of these providers because of their kindness and others for their cruelty. I remember being confused and I remember being afraid, but I do not remember making anyone cry. But apparently, I did.

I have told this story with laughter many times, even though the circumstances were not at all funny. For a while, the medical team was not sure I would survive. And after that, they were not sure I would return to my prior level of functioning. I use humor with this narrative because it enables me to feel a sense of ownership over the story. There are huge chunks of time I cannot account for—time that I do not remember clearly and only encounter through evidence in my journal, my medical record, in my physical environment, and in little bits of stories from other people.

I was the least popular person in the ICU because I was advocating for myself. I was one of the few able to speak and able to request care and assistance. I also had the privilege of an involved and loving family who served as fierce supporters on my behalf when I was unable to speak. I saw so many who suffered the ill effects of short-staffed, stressed-staff, COVID-related delays, and systemic ageism and ableism. These observations inform my work with older adults, amplifying the beliefs I already had about ethics of care.

Not long after regaining some stability from the first near-death experience, I learned how to be the most popular person in the ICU. I was home on our ranch alone for the first time since the encephalitis. Our home is a mile and a half up a rural one-lane road. A beautiful spot, up at one thousand feet with a view of the nearby mountain. It was just me and the dogs, parrots, cats, llamas, sheep, and chickens. Everything was going well, and I did not feel nervous about managing it all.

In the early afternoon, I set up my yoga mat and props for a class on Zoom with a favorite teacher. Before class started, I went into the house to feed the dogs. While I was preparing their dinner, I heard a package delivery at the front door. I walked out the front door in my fuzzy yoga socks, picked up the package, and turned around to the front door. BAM BAM! Two sharp pains—one on my right big toe, one on the top of my left foot. Shock. A moment of uncertainty about the source of pain and then I looked down to see a baby rattlesnake right on our front doormat. The front door was open and the two dogs were standing on the threshold.

I made an ungodly, indescribable sound. I could not reproduce it if asked, but I remember thinking that I had never made such a sound before in my life. Still holding the box, I pushed the dogs inside and slammed the front door. In a blur, I went out to the studio and got my cell phone. I called my mom, who was down in Southern California. No answer. I called my dad who was forty minutes away at work in Berkeley. No answer. I called my mom again, and slightly incoherent, I got the story out. I was standing between the studio and the house, balanced on my heels, feeling a strange sensation spreading from the bite points up my feet and legs. Mom hung up and called my neighbors. Dad called back. Within the next five minutes, three of my neighbors arrived—one scooped me up and we began driving to the hospital. The other two were on their way up the driveway as we left—we rolled down the windows and yelled—"Go kill the snake!"

Norm was the perfect person to drive me to the hospital—a former social worker, he kept me calm and kept me talking as we drove.

"Erin, I can drive really fast and drive through red lights if you want, but I also want you to stay calm. So just keep talking and describe what you are feeling."

We rolled through the stop signs but did not run red lights and we got to the ER in about fifteen minutes.

We called ahead to the ER and let them know I was coming in with two rattlesnake bites. Later, I would learn this is an essential step to surviving snakebites! Not every hospital has the antivenom and sometimes they need to coordinate getting it there from another hospital.

As we drove, I told my neighbor what I was feeling—a strange tingling feeling on my feet and legs and most concerning, in the roof of my mouth: "It feels like pins and needles in my hard palate!" I sat nervously leaning forward, as though I could hurry our driving by leaning my body in the direction we were traveling.

When we arrived at the hospital, they were waiting for me at the door. They got me into a room and started fluids right away. Before the toxicologist arrived, my other neighbors had texted a photo of the successfully smashed snake. The photo is another essential step I learned—photographic proof or validation of the type of snake. Having the photo enabled starting the antivenom treatment right away, rather than wasting time with tests to determine the snake species.

Antivenom treatment is not a small matter—when they brought the IV bag in, they also rolled the crash cart to just outside my room.

"Just a precaution," they assured me.

But they had to monitor closely for adverse reactions as they administered the treatment. Having already experienced a severe adverse reaction to a medication—the situation that led to the encephalitis, I was especially nervous. But the antivenom worked according to plan and the emergency department transferred my care to the ICU—in a room not far from where I spent many weeks over the winter.

Once I settled in, the toxicologist came to visit me again. My earlier experiences led me to ask about the worst possible outcomes in order to feel prepared. Snake venom contains many dangerous things—it is meant to immobilize the snake's prey. This nasty stuff is full of proteins, enzymes, and toxins including neurotoxins. They cause bleeding, inhibit clotting and damage the vascular system. They also bind to and damage nerves. My feet were swollen and red, the bite points were clearly visible. Every few hours, medical staff checked the swelling and the redness and drew lines on my skin to indicate areas of concern.

The toxicologist calmly told me that the worst-case scenario was a double amputation. He told me it was possible, but not probable, that I would need a fasciotomy to reduce the swelling and damage to my feet and legs. I felt queasy and afraid, but I was still glad that I asked.

After the conversation with the toxicologist I sat in my bed and drew my legs and feet. Thinking of a favorite quote from Frida Kahlo, "Pies, ¿para qué los quiero si tengo alas para volar? Feet, what do I need you for, when I have wings to fly?" I wrote in my journal: "I love you, Frida, but I need my damn feet!"

Creating art in my hospital bed helped me to stay as calm as possible. I documented what I was seeing and feeling. It pulled my focus away from worry and into the mixing of colors and satisfaction of creating. It reminded me about who I am.

So back to the popularity tips—the photo of the baby rattlesnake ended up being my ticket to ICU-elite status. Several people on every shift, including a janitor and a security guard, came by my room to see the photo: "I heard you survived two snakebites at once! And you have a picture of the snake?!" One of the things that saved my life also made me a celebrity in the ICU.

That second ICU stay also provided some healing for the medical trauma I experienced before. Waiting out my observation, I saw with an unswollen brain how chaotic the ICU can be. I witnessed things that people may not believe. And I walked out of there, a few days after the snake bites, with minimal lingering effects. I also had more empathy for my previous self.

When I tell the snake bites story, I feel a nerve zap at the bite spots. Not painful, but just a little reminder of what happened. The body remembers and sometimes it communicates in ways that transcend words. Sometimes I get memory zaps in the form of small vignettes from the first hospitalization: a kind chaplain who took me to have lunch on a hospital patio in the fresh air, a supportive neurologist who took an interest in my art journal, the man who kept the entire medical floor awake with his pacing and howling all night, the smell of the soap in the bathroom. Little reminders of what I went through during that terrifying time. As the brain swelling resided, I worried other people would see me differently, so I did not talk about it. But these are human experiences and not reasons for shame or secrecy.

Now, I step carefully and boldly into each day. My feet hold me up. I feel humbled by the resilience of my brain and this body—in awe of the many layers of survival. Sometimes I wish I had more stories, more information about the encephalitis. It is hard to ask questions of others as often as I want, because it was traumatizing for everyone else, too. So I laugh as I recount the stories I do have, and I share snakebite survival tips whenever I can, even though I feel it in my feet each time. This life I live now is not borrowed or a bonus, but rather hard-won. My self and my body fought hard to be able to tell these stories, laugh, and evolve into this new phase of my life.

3

ACT OF LOVE

Ana Mercedes Rivera-Pagan

My mother was a gifted seamstress. She was the type of artist who could look at the picture of a gown in a magazine and duplicate it, without a pattern. She also had an incredible gift for math, and it was her dream to go to college after she graduated from high school. Prior to the Spanish–American War of 1889, Puerto Rico was part of the Spanish Empire. For four hundred years schools were operated by the Catholic Church. Education was reserved for men if they had resources.

Women were ignored and had no rights. Some, if they were fortunate to have progressive male siblings, were taught by their brothers. My mother was born in 1925, long after the Spanish–American War ended, and the island was an American territory. Universal education was in place, but the cultural values of the Spanish regime still existed along with the patriarchy of American culture where society favored men.

And so, a brilliant mind was lost and confined to a factory situated in the garment district of Manhattan, an industrial area of the city that had seen better days. The district centered around Seventh Avenue just north of Penn Station. New subway lines connected the Lower East Side to the district, making it easy for buyers and manufacturers to visit factories.

Like all the workers, my mother was paid based on the number of units completed. Piece rate work did not come with health insurance, dental or vision care, sick leave, vacation, or time off.

I was a junior in high school, and it was the last day of our three-week summer enhancement program. It was an enrichment project that consisted of a book club, movies, theater excursions, and subject matter reviews, designed to prepare seniors for the Regents exams. I opted to review a few core classes in preparation for the Regents' exams in my senior year. I also signed up for the book club and theater excursions.

I was looking forward to visiting my aunts Titi Aida and Titi Lydia, my mother's sisters. They lived in the country where everything was green, and the temperature was cool. I loved spending the summers there, running through the fields and orchards and climbing trees.

I walked toward the bus stop in the oppressive heat. It was so hot it would cause blisters on your skin if you dared to touch anything that had soaked up the heat. Such summer days were harsh and often I suffered from heat rash, headaches, and nausea if exposed for any length of time. You could literarily see the waves of heat rising off the pavement and feel the sticky whoosh of your shoes as they lifted when you walked.

As I waited for the bus, I watched a man hurriedly commanding his dog to potty, oblivious to the hot asphalt that was burning his dog's paws. I thought, surely, he could feel the soles of his sneakers making the swoosh sound they make when fighting to release themselves from meltdown. A dog's paws are flesh not protected by shoes or sneakers. I heard the dog whining before the man realized his dog was in pain and thought to myself cruelty is both conscious and unconscious.

The few trees in sight were wilting. The humidity was high. My clothes were sticking to my body and there were no signs of shade to retreat to. Sweat trickled down my face and a slight headache was beginning to make its presence known when the bus finally arrived. It was a short bus ride to our apartment, but long enough in the air-conditioned bus for me to recover from the fatigue and discomfort caused by the heat.

In those days we lived in a two-family home. The building was a modified row house of attached and semi-detached three-story houses with faint art deco brickwork. We lived on the second floor above a retail store. Windows were present along the front of the house and the fire escapes lined the back.

Our apartment opened into the living room with the kitchen and our dining table to the right where my brother and I ate and did our homework. Past the living room there was a large bedroom separated from the living room by a beaded curtain; off to the left side was my room.

I could smell the food my mother was making before I opened the door. She was making arroz, which was rice with a chicken fricassee and garbanzos that I liked. I was surprised that she was home so early.

I said, "Bendicion, Mami," asking for her blessing.

She replied, "Que Dios te bendiga."

I countered with, "It's too early for you to be home. Is everything OK?"

She laughed and said, "El tiempo esta muy caliente y tuvemos que ir nos tempranos."

I said, "It's good that they let you out early, it is dangerously hot out there."

She had soft bolero music playing describing people in love, out of love, or longing for love. Boleros were soothing and sometimes brought tears to my eyes. She played the old artists. El Trio de Los Panchos was a favorite.

She played music when she was cooking. I did not know if it was common in all households, but my parents communicated with music. I always knew when they were fighting. The lyrics of the music told the story; often it had to do with my father's infidelities. Sometimes the music spoke of my mother's desire to escape the cultural and religious prison she lived in. Sometimes they were direct, and she was telling him to get out of her life.

The music on Saturdays was different. She and I danced and sang to the sounds of a rhythmic life she imagined and desired. She taught me how to dance to those rhythms. I think those rhythms became part of the flame that gave me wings.

My mother left the pot she was tending and came around to the front door and greeted me affectionately with an awkward embrace. Physical endearments were not easy for her. Orphaned at a young age, affection was unknown territory for her. I often wondered what had happened to her, but she never wished to speak of her life growing up. I collected bits and pieces by pretending I didn't understand Spanish well and while I did not have details at that time, I knew it was not good.

As she released me from her embrace she said, "I got you a job for the rest of the summer at the factory where I work."

Stunned silent, I found my voice after a long pause and quietly asked, "Mami, what do you mean you got me a job? I have been spending part of the summer with Titi Aida and Titi Lydia, in Buffalo since I was a child. You know I can't breathe here. It is not just the cooler climate and cleaner air. I need space, green, and open sky."

"Si, yo se, pero, you are no longer a child; soon you will be a senior and you will need money for college."

Smiling, she continued. "I asked my boss to take you on as extra help so you could earn money for college. You will be paid one dollar twenty-five an hour. Now let's eat dinner so we can relax a little before we get things ready for tomorrow. We have an early morning ahead of us. Sometimes it takes a long time for the train."

Morning arrived too quickly. There was no time for breakfast. We had a little cup of café con leche and ran out the door toward the subway. As usual, the train was crowded, and we had to wait our turn at the turnstile. People were pushing their way down the stairs to get to the platform they needed, shoving their way into packed cars without regard for the young, the old, or the infirm. From station to station you could smell the people around you. Some wore heavy cologne or perfume that deadened your sense of smell, and the closeness of bodies and sweat was sickening.

I was still in shock when we arrived at the factory at seven that morning. The factory floor was cluttered, there were boxes everywhere filled with cloth, along with machinery and rolling racks. We clocked in and I was handed over to the steam press operator. She casually pointed out the steps required for operating the machine and watched me as I followed her instructions. There were two types of pressing machines, one for pressing and one for ironing. The temperature or use of one or the other was determined by the item or fabric used.

Air conditioning did not exist, and the open windows invited a choking humidity that made breathing difficult. The cutters were stockpiling wool cloth for the sewing room, rotating fans filled the air with wool fibers that attached to our bodies because of the humidity, sweat, and steam.

My skin burned with a horrible itching. Angry red blotches formed on my arms, and I wanted to tear my flesh, yet I continued to work as directed. The heat was unbearable, yet everyone continued working.

Something awakened in me as I realized that this was my mother's daily reality. She and the others had no choice. If they didn't work, there would be no money, no food, no shelter.

The trip home was almost as wretched as the factory. It was rush hour and people pushed their way into crowded subway cars so tightly I couldn't move. During the morning rush, I noticed that people avoided eye contact or looked away into vacant space. During the evening rush hour you could see their eyes, weary and desperate.

Once in our apartment Mami had me strip and shower the wool dust off my body then rubbed lotion on my erupted skin. Dressed, I sat at the kitchen table processing the day's events. I knew we were poor but until that moment I did not understand the suffocating limitations my mother dealt with.

Walking over with plates of food she said, "You don't have to return to the factory tomorrow."

I stuttered, "I don't understand, you arranged the job for me, what do you mean I don't have to go back?"

She smiled, motioning that I should eat and replied, "Yes, I planned for you to work with me for one day so that you could see and feel the kind of future you would have if you didn't go to college. I wanted you to feel the heat, discomfort, and desperation of a dead end and understand that all work is honorable … but a life of desperation and vacant eyes is not for you."

I can say with all certainty that one act of love changed and cemented the entire trajectory of my life.

4

BEYOND THE GLITZ:
My Journey from Hollywood to Healing

Aria Johnson

I had finally made it in Hollywood, or so I thought. After more than a decade of chasing dreams as a singer, I received a call to star in a TV show called Beverly Hills Pawn.

"Can you bring five black dresses and be here at 5 a.m.?" asked the executive producer.

"Absolutely," I replied, my heart racing as I dashed to Nordstrom.

Music was my first love, and acting was never in my plans. But after quitting the music business and getting married, I figured I'd give being an entertainer one last try. "Just one year of auditions," I promised myself. And so, in twelve months, I filmed five pilots, all fizzling out until Reelz Channel picked one up for a thirteen-episode run. Suddenly, I was in a whirlwind: number one show on the network, a five-season contract, airing in eighty-three countries worldwide.

Talk shows, Hollywood billboards, endless parties, and red carpets became my world. It was all glitz and glam, but deep inside, I felt ... empty. I had transformed into a character, a caricature really, and the toxic set culture was palpable. Despite the eighty-hour weeks and constant fear of getting axed, I told myself, "Be grateful; you've finally made it!"

Yet, as the fifth season wrapped, I yearned for more—more life, more love, more joy. I wanted to start a family.

"None of the fame or money matters," I shared with my husband, Luke. "What matters is love, and I want to grow our love with a baby."

Luke was all in. His only condition? "Not in LA."

So we looked at a map and started dreaming. We decided on Bend, Oregon, a picturesque mountain town, to begin our new chapter.

Seasons six and seven loomed on the horizon, and I knew I could fly back to shoot if I wanted, but the truth was, my heart wasn't in it. Ironically, on our moving day to Oregon, news came in—the show was canceled, even though it was still in the number one spot. My stomach dropped … but not because I was disappointed. I felt a surge of relief that I could finally move on with my life. I felt, for the first time in a long time, peace.

To my shock and joy, I became pregnant right away with a baby girl, my dream come true. We named her Kailiana Blue, and she was the most beautiful angel I had ever seen. With my heart so full of love that I could hardly stand it, she was my everything, my whole world, and I felt as if I were standing on top of it. I regularly quoted the words, "The only thing that matters is to love and to be loved," and nothing proved this truer than being a mother.

Motherhood brought with it a familiar need to be an overachiever, a trait I've always possessed. I juggled being a full-time entrepreneur, a wife, a mom, and attempting to craft a Pinterest-perfect life. I felt I had to do it all. I didn't have "status" anymore, so I went over the top to prove that I was good enough.

Once upon a time in my twenties, I was a recording artist who won awards, opened for Ludacris, and sang to packed stadiums. But fame was never the goal. I yearned to move people's souls, to bring love, empowerment and change through music. I wanted to inspire people, so when I quit being an artist, I decided to help young singers make it in the music business. I launched The Golden Voice, a vocal coaching and artist development business. I was deeply committed to guiding these emerging talents on their artistic journey, empowering them to make a global impact. And the beauty of it all? I could coach via Zoom from Oregon.

But life in Bend wasn't without its challenges. We bought another house during a chaotic time. The week we moved, my husband was making history in Belize, filming for Discovery Channel's Shark Week and taking Richard Branson four hundred feet deep into the Blue Hole in a submarine; meanwhile, my nanny quit, and we hadn't yet sold the old house. I was stretched thin and trying to manage on little sleep. I remember giving myself a pep talk: "You are a superwoman; you can do this!" I was overwhelmed and didn't know how to ask for help, running on caffeine, adrenaline, and sheer will.

The day of the move was when everything went sideways. Luke was still on set, so I was alone with the movers, handling moving a six-bedroom house. As soon as he could, he caught the first flight home, and when he arrived, I collapsed. The stabbing pain in my stomach was worse than labor, and I thought I was going to die. I ended up in the ER, and since the doctor didn't know what was wrong with me, she said it was all in my head.

As time went on, pain became my constant companion. Every bone and muscle ached, and the neurological damage was so severe that I couldn't put sentences together. I felt incredibly dumb. I quit my job coaching singers because my throat was bleeding—there were days upon days when I couldn't talk. I'd fall asleep silently weeping from pain and wake up dreading the day. Every meal I ate caused the feeling of a heart attack; it was a living hell. I spent months and eventually years with doctors, and no one could help me. I was completely burned out.

And then came the darkest moment. I was driving on the freeway when a terrifying thought crossed my mind: "Kailiana and Luke would be better off without me. I should drive my car into this center divider."

It was the first and only suicidal thought I've ever experienced. In a state of utter shock, I called Luke. Reacting quickly, he reached out to my mother, who flew in and took me to a cabin in the woods. There, I endured a cold-turkey detox from a cocktail of pharmaceuticals, including antidepressants, anti-nausea meds for cancer patients, and Valium before every meal just to swallow food. All of which weakened my system. Years later, I would discover the medication for digesting food listed "suicidal ideation" as a side effect—a fact my doctor had neglected to mention.

For the record, I do not recommend abruptly discontinuing medication; it's a rough process. I chose this path out of fear and a deep-seated desperation to grasp at whatever straws were left, to fight for my life. I was so sick that I couldn't walk, crawling on my hands and knees to the bathroom. I didn't shower, I barely ate, I lay on the couch, and detoxed. I found myself consumed with anger at the world and God for subjecting me to such torment.

"I don't deserve to suffer like this; I'm a good person," I thought. "Why is this happening to me?" I'd ask, again and again.

I returned from that cabin in the woods determined to overhaul my thinking and signed up for a self-development conference. I figured I'd never get better unless I knew, without a shred of doubt, that healing was possible. I needed to reprogram my brain! I'd always had an interest in self-development, but at this point, I went all in, giving it 100 percent effort. I devoured books, listened to podcasts, attended seminars—you name it. I applied every technique with determination, on a quest for something, anything, that worked.

Fed up with the side effects of Western medicine, I sought the help of a functional physician. At one point, my regimen involved taking one hundred supplements per day. Despite my best efforts, I was still sick. I felt defeated, lost, and scared. I had become a shadow of my former self, but I couldn't give up; my daughter needed me. Using my love for her, I propelled myself forward. I was uncertain of how, but I knew I had to shift my mindset to heal.

The road to answers was long and winding—five years, twenty doctors, a series of invasive tests, a string of misdiagnoses, and a concoction of pharmaceuticals. The final diagnoses read like a horror show: gastroparesis (a paralyzed stomach), small intestinal bacterial overgrowth, severe GERD, leaky gut, adrenal fatigue, hypocontractile esophagus, hypothyroidism, mold poisoning, mercury poisoning, and chronic fatigue. It was beyond overwhelming. And to top it all off, I was diagnosed with generalized anxiety disorder and depression—hardly a surprise given the circumstances.

I had a choice: let the pain make me bitter or better. I chose better. I learned to shift perspectives, to stop asking, "Why is this happening to me?" and start exploring, "How is this happening for me?"

At first, I couldn't think of one good reason for the years of chronic pain and suffering. But then it clicked—my lifelong dream of helping others was entirely external, but how could I help people change their lives without having my own life-changing experience? This intimate dance with pain had a purpose.

These challenges were not roadblocks but stepping stones, shaping me into someone capable of empathizing, identifying, and guiding people through a path of recovery, so they can be not only successful, but happy and healthy. Now when people read my words or see me speaking on stage, I'm teaching them how to prevent and recover from burnout through self-love. But first, I needed to discover it for myself.

As a chronic people pleaser, I was accustomed to putting others' needs ahead of my own. I would please, perform, and perfect without a second thought. It occurred to me that to truly love myself, I had to take care of myself as I would a small child. This meant learning to eat when I was hungry, sleep when I was tired, and go to the dang gym, even when I didn't feel like it. I had to make self-care a nonnegotiable priority. "I'd never neglect to feed my child; why was I neglecting to feed myself?" I questioned.

And so, after countless doctors and thousands of pills, I realized the road to recovery both started and ended with me. I embraced 170-degree sauna sessions, complemented by guided meditation every day. This practice, particularly a "future-self meditation," became my beacon during the darkest times, a tool to tap into my inner wisdom. Post-sauna, I'd plunge into an ice bath (even though I hate the cold), building resilience while reducing inflammation in the body. I found journaling incredibly therapeutic, redefining my perspective of the past.

I revamped my approach to health and fitness, choosing to eat and work out not to look a certain way, but to nourish and strengthen my body. I incorporated breathing exercises and started and ended each day with gratitude exercises. The intricacies of how and why these techniques worked could fill an entire book—in fact, it's the subject of my speeches and workshops. But for now, I'll tell you what I've learned.

Reflecting on my journey, I see how the highs and lows have profoundly shaped me. Was it self-development or my relentless spirit that healed me? It's hard to say. Life's not perfect; I still monitor my nutrition, take supplements, and use some medications. Yet, the transformation is undeniable. I've found true happiness and discovered my authentic self.

I uncovered a version that's happier, more resilient, and just … more aligned with who I want to be. This is all thanks to my greatest challenge. Throughout this journey, I've learned that the quality of our lives hinges on the stories we tell ourselves and the meanings we give to our experiences. Remember, the power to choose is in our hands.

Looking back, I'm grateful for the pain; it sculpted me into someone I'm proud to be. And if I can do it, so can you. So, here's to finding your way, turning challenges into teachers, pain into power, and embracing life with joy and authenticity. Cheers to us and our journey, the amazing stories yet to unfold, and to each of us in our pursuit of greatness.

5

WHAT IS REAL LOVE?

Aman Gohal

It bubbles below the heart, a feeling of warm openness, aliveness, and wonder. Joy fills my body – radiance oozes from my pores as a soft glow, a natural smile rests on my face, and the spirit sparkles in my eyes. It is not a high, it's not a mood or momentary bliss nor is it tied to one person – love is aliveness of my being. And to be there –fully in the present, is to feel my creator's presence in and around me. How wonderful for the soul and terrifying for the ego. The story of the Skeleton Woman illustrates this quite well.

Below is a paraphrased version of The Skeleton Woman an Inuit Tale of Healing (adapted from *Women who Run with the Wolves: Myths and Stories of the Wild Woman Archetype* by Clarissa Pinkola-Estes, ©1992, 1995, 1996)

A woman was thrown over a cliff by her angry father after doing something he disapproved of. Her beautiful body sank to the bottom of the sea and was devoured by flesh eating fish. A fishermen's line hooked into her rib cage. He was ecstatic with the weight of the catch – imagining what it could be...only to be terrified to see the Skeleton Woman. The Skeleton Woman was also terrified. The more they fought in fear to free themselves the more tangled in the line they became. The fisherman quickly rowed to the shore, jumped out of his boat and tried to run away from her – unaware that she was entangled and running right behind him. He finally found a warm cave and burned a fire to discover the Skeleton Woman right next to him. This time with patience and care he started to untangle and unhook the fishing line. Staying up most of the night to do so... he eventually dozed off into a sleep. As he dreamt, he shed one tear ...a tear of sadness and longing. The Skeleton Woman drank the tear and her thirst was filled. She then took out his heart – the great drum and started to play it. She sang for flesh as she played, and flesh returned to her body. She was restored to her original form. She drummed more to sing his soul back to love and returned the great drum back inside the body of the sleeping fishermen and lay next to him. They woke up skin to skin, connected to one another.

Real love requires more fertile internal grounds that we must patiently tend to and cultivate. Diving into real love is becoming authentic which involves enduring hardships, challenges and having our edges (and fantasies) rubbed away.

The story of the Skeleton woman shows that an inner union is necessary for healing and experiencing a deeper love in the outer world. For that union we must reconcile the internal masculine and feminine we drank in early on in life that has us in endless unconscious patterns. It is in the crashing waves of reality against egoic fantasies that momentarily wake us and reminds us we are swimming in illusion (maya).

To put it simply in love is mutual blossoming not scraping for water in another's dessert. After being parched for decades, I recall an experience of inner love like a tiny...tiny point in the center of my physically and emotionally wrecked heart. One night I was enduring a self-berating voice that would not stop. An inner tormenter that I drank in a long time ago. After being beaten and worn down I heard a quiet whisper, "I see you as courageous. I see you as brave."

Those loving words brought tears to my eyes to know a deeper source of grace is available inside with unconditional love that can break through unconscious forces. It was not "self-talk" or any form of "self-help or self-determinism." It was a spring that rose up. I am a whole human made by a loving creator. Afterall, when we are connected to the reservoir of love… what skeletons can remain?

6

RECOVERING INTELLECTUAL

J. Mark Meadows

I was only five when my first taste for the intellect took hold. I remember my mom taking me to the Thayer Memorial Library in Lancaster, Massachusetts, a quintessential New England library with brick construction, stone columns, and ivy-framed windows. The experience was a thrilling rush—like the first time I tasted a warm apple cider donut covered in sugar and cinnamon.

The part of the library that sparked my imagination and curiosity was the spiral iron staircase that led to a narrow balcony of books, cordoned off with a chain. In my young, imaginative mind, I wondered what dusty books, treasures, and curiosities lay on the other side. I instinctively knew it wasn't a place I would be allowed as a kid.

There were old wooden reference tables, the scent of thick yellow pages, and the crinkle and feel of the books wrapped in protective plastic. My mom let me pick a handful of books and we'd settle into the chairs near the windows. The world seemed enormous and beautiful, and this gloriously mysterious place was a gateway to unknown worlds. I was enthralled and overwhelmed and wondered if it would be possible to read all the books in the library and what it would be like to know that much.

The allure of intellectual life was potent not only for the haven it provided but also for a sense of self-worth. Even if other people had more money, more security, and stability, I could feel equal to them if I was smart and well-read enough. I felt special, even above average, when I read Thoreau, Emerson, and Hawthorne the summer before my junior year of high school. I wanted to inhabit the world Thoreau described in Walden.

It wasn't just in my personal life that an analytical orientation to the world was important. As I entered the professional world of work in college admissions and later, executive recruiting and consulting, I learned the value of my intellectual currency. I could see patterns in human behavior and organizational systems. I developed new models and insights that clients and colleagues praised. As I continued to hone this strength and explore immense intellectual seas, I unwittingly lost sight of the shores of emotion, intuition, and mystery. This charming and rewarding life of the mind, which started so innocently, began to feel more like a prison than a refuge. I felt my intuition atrophy. My emotions became constrained. My relationships thinned. The world that seemed infinite as I explored it through my intellect began to shrink because I had tried to bind it to a single dimension.

I knew I didn't want to live the rest of my life as an intellectual, skewed toward an oversimplified way of understanding and being in the world. So, in a lurching and sometimes plodding way I have been reclaiming this place of curiosity and spontaneity, of play and learning. As a result, I am coming back to myself.

I return when I see the world through my kids' eyes. I remember to inhabit the world more fully as I practice mindfulness and ground my attention in my body, breath, and the present moment. The world feels alive and wondrous again when I connect with my closest friends and spend time in nature. Music electrifies me and gives me goose bumps. I no longer need to invite my intellect into every experience, to name each piece of music, its composer, or key signature. It is enough to feel the music and know that the world is so much fuller and richer than any intellectual construct. This is my unlearning.

My journey through this internal landscape is one I experienced on a journey to Europe as I took my mom on a post-COVID vacation. While we were traveling, I was struck by my return to a purely instinctual, childlike curiosity. From the back of St. Vitus Cathedral in Old Prague, I was awestruck by the soaring Gothic ceilings, kaleidoscopic stained glass, and the gravitas of seven hundred years of history. My agnosticism was no match for the sacredness of the space as I felt a quiet reverence. Rather than thinking about the experience or trying to make sense of it through words and knowledge, I wanted to know this place in my bones, in my heart. I wanted to feel and experience the sublime directly, without the intermediary of my mind trying to comprehend and interpret.

Then, I noticed my mom just inside the doors of the cathedral. Her head was bowed, not out of reverence, but to examine a pamphlet detailing the extensive history of the cathedral. After what seemed an interminably long time, I asked her if she wanted to walk around and take in the cathedral instead of just reading about it—after all, we were eight thousand miles from home, why not soak up the experience? I asked her if she wanted to take the brochure with her to read later and she acquiesced. Toni Morrison's words ambled into my mind just at that moment. "At some point in life, the world's beauty becomes enough. You don't need to photograph, paint, or even remember it. It is enough."

My reaction to my mom's way of being in a new and unfamiliar place and the way she chose to initially experience it exposes my recovering intellectual self. I want to be the person who looks up at the cathedral, at the immensity of the sky, at the world. I want to be the young soul who stands speechless in amazement, rather than trying to catalog and accumulate as many facts as possible. This is me coming back to who I am. This is Mark, the mystic who loves questions more than answers.

Another place where I'm letting more of my intellectual and analytical self recede into the background is on my bike. For thirty years I've recorded and analyzed most of my rides—looking at distance, speed, heart rate, wattage, and other data. This analysis and tracking have helped me improve my fitness, perform competitively in events, and motivate myself. I've reached the point, perhaps based on age and experience, where I still track this information but am rediscovering the joy of simply riding my bike.

Two recent rides have been with my fourteen-year-old son. Sometimes I see how he pushes himself and other times how he coasts and savors the scenery. Watching him, I am inspired. The way he experiences cycling reminds me of what I used to enjoy: the sense of freedom, exploration, and possibility.

As was true inside St. Vitus Cathedral and Mom's study of a brochure, why would I stare down at my cycling computer to gauge my average speed, distance, altitude, and so on when I could look up at the magnificence that is everywhere around me? My senses bring me back to the present moment and riding for its pure, playful pleasure. I love the feeling of sunshine on my brown skin, the rush of warm summer air brushing my face, the smell of the tall grasses growing along the banks of the Sammamish River.

Through these experiences, I remember the fullness and wholeness of who I've always been. There will always be an intellectual who lives inside me, the five-year-old who loves the library and can't wait to settle into an afternoon of reading. What I know now and want to tell that wonderful kid is to also leave the library. Bolt across that threshold and out into the immense, beautiful world that always awaits. The world that can't be contained or reduced by thought, only felt, lived, and experienced. It is a world that may feel chaotic and scary but is also full of love, delight, and mystery and I want to embrace it all!

7

DON'T BE AFRAID OF THE WOLF

Yukiko Amaya

Miracles abound in my life now. There are messages coming in from the Mother Goddess, the Divine Source, through trees and birds, water and air, through the earth and stones. But it was not always like this.

No … I think of those dark, dark days in my late thirties when my father was dying a slow and painful death from cancer in Tokyo, and my husband with whom I had built a life in Los Angeles, told me he was leaving me for a "better woman."

I could not sleep, and I could barely function, but would pull myself together to go and produce yet another TV commercial shoot on location somewhere out in the world. Nothing made sense and I wanted to just disappear and fade away. My whole world was collapsing around me, and I could not see a way through.

One day, while I was back in Tokyo tending to my dying father in hospital and completely exhausted from lack of sleep, I pulled over by the side of the road. I could not drive an inch further. My father had been in a coma for over a month, and I could see him hanging in there only by a thread. The sheer grief over his suffering and his imminent loss engulfed me. There, on a side street in Tokyo, I curled up into a small ball inside my parents' Honda Accord and howled and wept my fear, my rage, my hurt, my grief, my confusion and utter panic at losing the one parent who was the one I could communicate with. Who was the one I had chosen to emulate. After a long while, numb from all the tears and rage unleashed, I lay there, alone in the car, sucking on my thumb and shuddering occasionally.

It was at that moment that a scenery so vivid I could have sworn I was right there, unfolded before me. I was lying in the white snow. It was freezing. Everything was white. The sky was heavily clouded, hanging low with snow silently falling.

"This is where I die" was a random thought that came and went. I felt sad I was leaving this life, my existence here on earth, so alone and so cold.

Far in the distance was a dark line of trees. A forest. Then out of that forest came something, moving toward me. As it grew closer, I could see that it was an enormous wolf.

"This is how I die," I thought.

I had no energy or will left in me to try and run. So, I simply watched this wolf coming closer and closer until it stood right by me staring into my eyes with her piercing grey eyes. I closed my eyes wondering if this would hurt. I felt her breath on me, then this giant she-wolf did the unthinkable. She lay down and wrapped herself around me. She let me suckle on her, keeping me warm with her radiating heat and fierce protection. I had never ever been held in that kind of care and belonging. I felt so safe that I fell asleep in her embrace. A dreamless sleep so healing I woke up with new energy and clarity.

I grew up in a highly educated, middle-class family in Tokyo, Japan. I was the middle child and the only girl sandwiched between my two brothers. My father was a career bureaucrat, and my mother was a housewife. They were both quite liberal-minded and despite their reservations about my being a girl, and a very independent-minded one at that, mostly left me to my own devices. I decided quite early on that it was my father who had more independence and power compared to my mother. I resolved to be more like him. I practiced speaking like a man (or how I identified my father spoke), never speaking fanciful or dreamy, always with logic, science, and data to back up my words. Well, that was my aspiration.

With that modus operandi in place, I set out to carve out a place for myself in the world. I left Japan as soon as I graduated from university and went to Paris, France, to figure out if I was made of a resilient enough material to make it by myself out in the "real" world. I refused all financial assistance from my parents and found my way in Paris. Then at the age of thirty-four, I fell in love and found myself moving from Paris to Los Angeles to be with my boyfriend (who became my future, second ex-husband). By this time, I had left my beloved modern dance and choreography behind so I could get a "real" job and make a proper living. I fell by chance into a world of filming Japanese television commercials in various locations internationally. It was very much a man's world at the time. Despite that, it turned out that I was very good at producing these huge jobs with big male egos flying around.

But there were consequences to the work. I completely ignored what I ate and smoked like a fiend. I was not getting much sleep as I coordinated between Japan and the US and Europe and Australia as the job dictated and was living one-third of my year on planes and in hotels. My first health crisis came in my late twenties when I developed a huge cyst on my right ovary. They took out the entire ovary with the cyst. In my early thirties, I developed another cyst on my left ovary. I did not want to go back under the knife after the horrible experience I had with the surgical removal of my right ovary. So I decided to heal it energetically with a team of energy healers I "ran into" in Paris. One woman did healing work with her stones. Another with herbs, and the third member of the team was an osteopath. In three months, my hard, large egg-sized cyst disappeared completely to the utter bafflement of the medical doctors.

From that experience alone, I knew there were energies and realities that were beyond my five senses, that could reach into this material world and effect shifts and changes even in my body. But it did not occur to me that I could "enter into" this other reality. I had no clue what it was. I was simply a recipient.

That day, in the Honda on a side street in Tokyo was the beginning of a new reality for me. This time, there were no healers around. It was just me. The huge grief and trauma of what was happening in my world had somehow weakened the dividing wall between my "waking world" reality and "dream time" reality and created a portal into what the Celts call the "Otherworld." I soon realized that I could access this Otherworld almost at will. I could go there anytime and call upon the She-wolf to come and cuddle me, and she would. It was a lifesaver.

Have you had experiences like that? Or dreams that felt more real than real, that helped shift your "reality" and brought you deeper comfort or understanding in the end? We all have different entry points, and they are specific to our life lessons of the soul. No one way is better or worse. We may have preferences, but that is all.

Over the months that followed the experience with the She-wolf, it was as if the separating wall between waking reality and the Otherworld became very porous. After my father's passing, at his second funeral put on by the research institute he had been the head of, he showed me his soul leaving his body as waves of light. It happened a few weeks after his body was cremated and his ashes were in an urn. He then spoke to me as his funeral carried on, and showed me an amazing vision of the flight of the soul as a beautiful crane. I saw it as if I were right there in this peaceful, alpine environment. A beautiful and still lake lay surrounded by forest and high mountain peaks. Mist floated above the lake. Out of the mist came a giant crane who glided down toward the surface of the lake and with his talon traced a line on the water. "This is the trace of our life on this earth," my father said. As the crane flew off, he said, "And the soul keeps on going forever."

I have never forgotten that moment. My father who had been agnostic in his life came to me as a soul to show me things after his passing. He literally opened up my psychic and shamanic potential and from that moment on, sent me teachers.

In order to help me cope with my grief, a friend of mine gave me a book before I left Tokyo for Los Angeles that had helped him when he lost his wife to cancer. I don't remember the name of the book, but it was about a shamanic way of journeying to receive healing from trauma and grief. What I do remember is they suggested I set aside a specific time to grieve each day, so that I could still function enough to carry on my daily life of work and living. That was what I did.

Back home in Los Angeles, I sat at my altar for the first of these "grieving journeys." The moment I sat down and closed my eyes, I was suddenly presented with a visual of a house on a hill with a well beside it. Curiosity drew me to the well. I looked in and knew I needed to jump in. I sank to the bottom of the well where I located a trapdoor. I swam through that door and came up into an underground cavern. There was a path dimly lit. I followed it to a door in the rock wall. It opened into a large hall with a ceiling so high it disappeared into the gloom. The room itself was flooded with light coming from high, gothic windows. The floor was paved with large squares of black-and-white marble in a checkered pattern. Enormous columns rose out of the floor.

From behind a column emerged a man dressed in a deep green cape with a large hood drawn over his head. I could not see his face, but he came quickly up to me and said, "What took you so long?" Then, taking my hand, led me to the throne at the end of this hall, and seated me there.

For many months, I would visit him and be taught lessons about life and how to see. It was extraordinary and the beginning of a complete shift in my life and awareness. This was the beginning of my training in yoga and shamanism.

This beginning taught me that what I thought was "real" was an incredibly limited understanding and vision of life, largely dictated by culture, societal contracts and agreements. It also showed me that the invisible world existed right alongside the visible one, and the access point was everywhere. One just has to pay attention and be open and patient. I experienced the expanded world as that of great compassion and kindness and love.

It took many years of various teachers and mentors and trainings, both of this world and the Otherworld, to start to gain more clarity. I realized over time that wisdom is not outside but within each of us, as is the source of love. It seems that when we look for "quick fixes," we can fall into deception and manipulated realities of others that do not consider what is for our highest good. I also know now that whatever challenges come our way, it is a huge portal into breaking through and beyond old beliefs that are holding us captive.

I now trust myself to walk each step, especially through the dark, underground places. Help is right there by my side.

8

WAKING UP IN BALI

Joy Dyanne Stearns

"It is not down in any map; true places never are."
– Herman Melville

I lay in my modest Balinese cottage in the early morning light with a smile stretched across my face. There was a cacophony of sounds: Distant voices, puttering motors, a nerve-bending saw … and yet the sounds were that of a holy moment. There were crickets and birds with a dash of gecko. It was perfect.

I stretched my way out of bed, wrapped a sarong around my waist, and walked barefoot across the tile floor of my open-air dwelling. I steeped some jasmine leaves and sliced a papaya as the fresh new day held me. Taking my comfortable seat, in profound peace, I sipped my tea, simply listening, beginning to tune into my morning spiritual practice. As I opened my eyes, Ibu walked through the gate, with today's offering flowers. Her morning routine was to sweep fallen leaves from the yard clearing out the old, welcoming the new.

What I considered traveling smart turned out to be a meticulously orchestrated gift. A trip to Bali was a blend of divine timing and frequent flier miles delivering me to one of the most sacred destinations on earth. Bali was a soft place to rest between Western life in the US before heading back to the Eastern life I had started in Kathmandu. I was nervous to return to the sacred place where my healing journey began. Fortunately, my flat was rented, my annual independent work was completed and I was able to have some freedom for the first time in my adult life.

How on earth did I end up here, a honeymoon destination by myself? How does a divorced woman, a single mother "empty nester" end up on the other side of the globe, trekking on full moon pilgrimages with a shaman and dancing barefoot in sacred temple gardens? I was literally and metaphorically between clothing sizes, between homes and time zones, and between heartbreaks.

When packing in Santa Fe for my indefinite trip to the East, the remainder of my late daughter's ashes somehow ended up in a small glass container in my suitcase. My child of five had died in a horrific, devastating accident more than a decade before. I simply did not know what to do with the rest of her ashes. So far none of my attempts to release her remains seemed grand enough to truly honor her life or to assuage my pain. At the time it didn't dawn on me that I would be in Bali for the Solstice, a holy day, her late birthday.

In the aftermath of Malia's passing, I managed to launch her older brother from the nest and into college. I was exhausted from the trauma of it all and my body, mind, and soul craved respite. I had made it this far without a nervous breakdown, but the cracks were beginning to appear. I had been in counseling and medicated to maintain a certain level of order, to function at work, and to keep a roof over our heads. "OK, Mama," life seemed to say, "We've made it this far without a nervous breakdown. It's high time to fall completely and utterly apart."

Suddenly random symptoms popped up, the worst being unpredictable bouts of vomiting. My doctors ordered extensive tests, avoiding the "C-word," in an attempt not to scare me. I was scared, terrified actually, that I would die before getting to go anywhere or do anything that I wanted with my life. I had outlived one child, trying to make a decent life for the other simply living in survival mode working jobs I hated. I had wasted my precious time attempting relationships with noncommittal, avoidant, and unavailable men. I had not done anything creative, expressive, or even meaningful for me. I realized that I did not want to die an unlived life.

Now in Bali, preparing my daily offering, I held the ever so slightly peach ivory petals of a delicate rose. They fell off of my hand. As I held them, I inhaled, breathing deeply. Upon exhalation, my eyes filled with tears, reminded of the hundreds of the pale peach, ivory, and softest pink rose petals that my sister and I carefully plucked to cover my daughter's cold little body before cremation.

I clutch, gripping this experience, the sublime beauty of these petals, in the same way I could not let go of her ashes. My soles met the carpet of green cooled by the dew that had also polished the broad leaves of the tropical plants bordering the garden.

Tiptoeing across the grass I made my way on the path behind my little abode to make my morning offering. I place tiny flowers arranged in bamboo trays at the base of the family shrine, allowing the flowers to sing the intention, their language of beauty, sounding notes of glorious color, eloquent songs ringing from each petal and leaf. I am offering the sacred scent of some of the flowers of my upbringing, placing rose, tuberose, and gardenia for the three offerings to the holy trinity. These precious essences have left behind an indelible etheric scent imprinted on me from the wise woman lineage of my mother, my grandmothers, and my ancestors. These superpower flowers have emitted their intoxicating aroma for our family's birthdays, weddings, and funerals.

When I arrived in Bali, my driver gave me a Balinese name. When I told him my child had died, he was genuinely sorry, since his mother died when he was a boy.

"I am going to name you Ibu," he said. "It's important and respectful; Ibu means mother."

After he dropped me off at my guest house, I introduced myself as "Ibu," letting the owner know I was en route back to Nepal where I had been named "Ananda Devi."

She exclaimed, "Ibu Devi it is!"

Her smile turned into a frown as she listened to my misfortune, the sad news that my child died, and later my husband. When I mentioned I had my late daughter's ashes with me the tone turned somber.

"What do you mean, ashes?" she said.

"My daughter's ashes are in my suitcase," I replied.

"Here, with you? In your room?!"

I was in an awkward predicament. I learned quickly that it was taboo to have ashes in Bali, if not blatant superstition, since it would bring bad luck to anyone with them. It was a terrible imposition for the family and the driver who had driven me and, unknowingly, the ashes. My host started calling to coordinate an expensive funeral. I was expected to pay their priest for a ceremony to say prayers to clear the negativity of "dirty ashes."

Before getting completely swept out to sea with Malia's ashes in a ceremony that did not feel like my own, I called my friend, Mogli, another driver I had met, desperately seeking answers. I pleaded with him to find out who could shed some light on the unwelcome presence of these ashes. They wanted me to stay, to pay more. But I had to leave. I was on my way to Tibet. I had to leave Bali safely with my daughter's ashes.

Mogli drove me to a village to visit a local priestess. She spoke English and explained it was not my problem. She said that the owners of the guest house did not post any rules or restrictions. She promised to send a Monku with holy water for a ceremony of my own. The next day after a brief and heated exchange in Bahasa with the guesthouse owner, Mogli moved me, my bags, and ashes to my new abode.

Mogli drove me to collect traditional offerings for my daughter's ceremony. First stop, a shop for traditional sarongs and lace blouses. My daughter whispered in my ear, wanting the most expensive. As we drove away, I fretted over it until I saw a sign, literally, a big yellow smiley face with her name on it. "You didn't have to buy me a prom or a wedding dress," I felt/heard her say. "I want this one, Mama," she insisted.

I went back and bought it. Mogli and I visited a village specializing in silver filigree where I bought bracelets and rings. A sparkly rainbow offering basket practically hopped off of the shelf at a local market. We laughed knowingly as I chose fresh flowers, fruit, and incense. I was delighted as we drove through a village of kite makers where we stopped to buy a vibrant blue butterfly and a bright green dragon. "Kites are not tradition," Mogli said.

"So what?" I replied. "It's our ceremony."

It didn't occur to me that I would be in Bali for Solstice, a holy day. I intended to disburse Malia's ashes on her late birthday, which turned out to be the Winter Solstice in this hemisphere. I shifted from left brain to right, from summer to winter, from Yin to Yang, Barang to Durga. In a beautiful ceremony of our making, I released the ashes into the ocean with blended intentions of love and mercy. I happily flew my butterfly kite. A profound burden that I didn't even know I had been carrying was lifted.

Afterward, I magically floated from one village ceremony to the next and was awestruck, humbled by the beauty of similar rituals, and offerings not unlike what I had done for my own child after she died. I was the most struck by the love notes, wishes, and prayers tucked in with the remains of loved ones before cremation.

My sister set up a Skype call so my mother and I would be able to see each other for her eighty-fifth birthday. Wrapped in a sarong, I walked barefoot through the garden giving her, my sister, and my grandniece a tour. Three generations of my family women were "oohing and aahing" over seeing me in such lush surroundings. Beaming on screen, my face was shining, plump, and dewy from the humidity.

"Thank you for my life, Mama. Without you, I wouldn't exist or even be here in this paradise."

Her eyes sparkled. "You are my joy. My birthday is happy just seeing how happy you are. How did you ever come up with this?"

Chuckling I said, "My best guess is that it's God's divine plan. I have not even had a chance to get a map or guidebook yet. Can you believe it?"

She said, "If you do, you just may miss something, especially if you are trying too hard to figure it out." She added, "Now you have the opportunity to learn to communicate without words."

Later that afternoon I slipped out of my sandals, onto my grass dance floor. I was elated to see my mom on her birthday, I was imbibing bliss and dancing like no one was watching until someone was. Jiwe's ten-year-old son was milling about his chores, sweeping dead blossoms and debris off of the lawn. He kept peering at me around the bushes.

Waves of self-consciousness crept in, and my thoughts started to trip me up. "He must think I'm crazy, some nutjob tourist." I curbed my thoughts and continued to surrender to the joy of dance.

I suddenly just wanted to BE. To let myself experience this joy. To let the beautiful, shy boy see what it is to be free. He distracted me, pulling me from my reverie. Coming back down to earth, my thoughts were practical with the need for him to empty my kitchen bin because gnats were attracted by the fruit rinds. I skipped toward my little villa and what I saw next stopped me in my dancing tracks.

This dear boy had collected fresh plumeria blossoms and placed rows of them across the stone steps of my entry. He had left an offering for me. He was nowhere to be seen. To my complete surprise, taking in his sweet gesture, I hung my head and wept in humility. He was not judging me; he was honoring me. It dawned on me that he had seen me dancing in the garden and in his own innocence and curiosity, he was generous with his offering of beauty. It was easy, natural, and all he knew. His cultural conditioning was to see and honor life, beauty, and the gods through offerings. He did not yet have any context for "crazy tourists," which was my own self-limiting belief. My mind's negative self-talk was the one judging me, nobody else.

When my daughter died it took me thirteen years to die to my old self and to essentially wake up in heaven in this blissful paradise. I was no longer running on the thoughts, beliefs, and experiences of my old life and false self. After more than a decade of grieving and laboring over the loss of my daughter, I was giving birth to my true self, awakening to my innate divinity. Golden sun reflects on the bottom of jungle leaves, effervescent green teaming with life. A blossom floated down from a tree blessing me.

9

JOINING HIS WORLD

Janet Lawson & Dan Swearingen

We never expected to be the parents of an autistic child, nor would we ever have dreamed that we would one day create a program for autistic teens and adults. When we were younger, had someone asked us, "What do you want to be when you grow up?" we would have answered:

"A writer."

"A physicist."

"An actress."

"A model railroad builder."

"A movie director."

"A fighter pilot."

Like many adults, we have ended up a long way from our early notions. It would never have occurred to us that the correct answer would turn out to be "creators of innovative ways of working with autistic teens and adults and operators of a nonprofit that specializes in helping them be more independent." In hindsight, our personal histories include many experiences that led us in this direction and made us ideally suited to develop the program we run today.

While inventing our program might have taken special skills and experience, we feel that the processes and techniques we use are rooted in common sense and good parenting and these can be used by any family, school, or program once the basic principles are understood. What follows is a narrative of how the program developed and points where we look back and realize that key insights came from particular personal experiences.

Janet spent her twenties studying acting, writing, performing theater pieces, and leading acting workshops. During those years, having children and being a mom were not on her agenda. But the work she did in those years shaped the mother and psychotherapist that she became.

One of the first lessons Janet learned in acting workshops was that the primary task of an actor is to listen intently to the other actors on stage. Listen with your whole body to the verbal and nonverbal messages from your colleagues. She learned that to truly listen she had to silence her internal voices and restless body. A director once yelled, "Shut your toes!" as she stood barefoot on stage wiggling her toes in anticipation of her next line. Letting go of her internal dialogue allowed her to connect to her fellow actors and to respond instinctively and naturally rather than simply following a script.

Meryl Streep once said that "acting is not about being someone different. It's finding the similarity in what is apparently different, then finding yourself in there." In that way, you become one with the character and view the world through their eyes. This way of connecting became the foundation for Janet's mothering and her practice as a therapist.

Dan grew up in San Francisco in the 1960s and early '70s and later a bit further north in Sonoma County in the '70s and '80s. Like his father, he was always fascinated with machines and gadgets. As a teenager he learned model building, electronics, carpentry, and auto mechanics.

Dan studied physics at the local state college and joined the US Marine Corps Reserve, planning to become an officer and pilot.

However, at this point he suffered several years of severe failure. Looking back, Dan can now say, "That's where I had the same kind of massive failure many of the students we work with today have suffered in their twenties—because I'm autistic." But he did not know that at the time.

He flunked out of college, lost all rank in the service, and skirted homelessness. He dug out slowly, worked a series of fast-food, retail, and blue-collar jobs. After several years Dan returned to college part-time resuming his study of physics. He met Janet and together we moved to Bloomington, Indiana, so he could work toward a PhD in astrophysics. He did not finish this degree. He left school ABD (all but dissertation). His PhD dissertation research was developing software and processes to analyze spectra from interacting binary star systems (Doppler Tomography with Cataclysmic Variables). Turning complex data into images gives insight into the structure of these complex systems.

While at Indiana University Dan taught astronomy courses and tutored local high school students in math and science. He had a reputation as a tough teacher, but his students did well, and he enjoyed figuring out ways to teach and explain complex subjects.

After a decade of traveling, graduating from UC Berkeley (magna cum laude), and various theater and film experiences, Janet spent her thirties getting clean and sober. She had several years of sobriety when she met Dan. In Bloomington while Dan worked on his PhD, she led Alateen meetings as part of her sobriety regimen. Every Monday night for five years Janet sat quietly and listened as teenagers told their stories of struggle with drug and alcohol addiction—their own and their families. She found she loved working with teenagers. She resonated with their struggles for independence, their search for identity, and above all, their brutal honesty. It was her work with these teens that led her to consider becoming a therapist.

While living in Bloomington, leading Alateen meetings, working at the town library, and on her master's in library and information science, Janet became pregnant. Toward the end of the pregnancy, Janet's blood pressure started to increase and she was diagnosed with preeclampsia. As her due date approached, her doctors worked to induce a normal delivery. After nearly two weeks, Janet's condition deteriorated to eclampsia and Ian was delivered by emergency C-section. Ian was full-term and a very healthy baby at birth.

In grad school after Ian's birth, we found it much more difficult to continue financially and Dan was starting to lose confidence he would ever be able to secure good employment as a college professor or an astrophysicist. We had done several contract projects testing early "multimedia PC" software products and writing user manuals for them. At that time, there was a new wave of tech start-ups using the Internet in the San Francisco Bay Area. Dan left graduate school in 1997 and immediately found work using his programming skills in this thriving arena that would later be called the dot-com boom. He learned the art of translating customer ideas into workable software and quickly became a team lead and then technical manager and manager of programmers.

Ian's Diagnosis

Back home in the San Francisco Bay Area, the months passed, and Ian continued to develop physically on track but his speech development was noticeably below average. We had one of those What to Expect When ... books and noted with increasing worry and dread each "normal" milestone he missed. He did not babble in a speech-like way in the early months. He was not drawn to noise-making toys, nor did he imitate different speech sounds. He seemed totally mystified by games of peekaboo. But he always smiled. He made eye contact. And he loved to be held. Ian seemed to communicate without words. And though we thought his utter fascination with cupboard door hinges, the pliability of a sheet of paper, or the concentric ripples in a dog's water dish was a bit eccentric, we simply chalked it up to being the son of a scientist. We took comfort in the stories that Einstein didn't speak until he was three years old. Even though Ian never measured up to the What to Expect When timelines he nevertheless developed into an attractive, engaging, and affectionate child.

Halloween 1997. Ian is two and a half years old and dressed as the color green for his nursery school party. But first a quick trip to the pediatrician for a well-baby check and health report required by the school. At the doctor's office, Ian is lost in his solitary play, enraptured by the motion of the hinges on the plastic playhouse in the waiting room. And we have been waiting. A long time. Young families come, are seen, and then go. A short, bespectacled man peers in periodically, watches Ian intently, and then leaves.

The nurse tries to record Ian's vital statistics—height, weight, eye-tracking. "He is not comfortable with strangers," Janet warns her as Ian's eyes widen, his arms stiffen, and his back begins to arch.

Janet holds Ian's hand while he steps onto the scale. But the unsteadiness of the small metal platform triggers a feral response. He leaps off and burrows into her legs, his face pressed so hard against her thighs that the seam of her jeans leaves an impression on his cheek.

"What if I hold him and we weigh in together? Then I will weigh alone and you can jot down the difference." Janet confuses the nurse but she agrees. When we get that sorted out the short man with the round glasses returns. This time he beckons us to follow. He reads from a clipboard a long list of questions: When did your son first roll over, crawl, walk, speak a word, a phrase? How does he interact with others?

And Janet responds honestly—physical development was right in line with the What to Expect When books. But the language development is still not there. She did not mention that she threw the What to Expect When books away as they in no way reflected Ian's growth. He developed outside their timeline—outside the norm.

Having gathered his data, a deep frown pulled at the doctor's lips but his brown eyes softened as he turned to Janet. "I believe your son is autistic."

The world stops. Somewhere deep in the center of her mommy's heart, Janet sighed with relief. This made so much sense.

With Ian's autism diagnosis and seeing the huge amount of support he needed we realized, one setback at a time, that caring for an autistic child was a full-time endeavor. Janet gave up trying to have a career and concentrated on creating a quiet, nourishing environment for Ian. As parents of autistic children know only too well, this was a round-the-clock job.

Ian began a school-based program for young autistics, and this allowed Janet to go back to school for another degree. This time in counseling psychology. Her goal was to learn as much as she could about how Ian's mind worked and to share this knowledge with other families to help them understand their autistic children.

As we figured out how to raise Ian, there were several key events that, in hindsight, we see taught us very important lessons in our understanding of autism and how to support and encourage autistics.

Joining His World

When Ian was very young (three to four years old) he had very little language. However, he would sing songs and recite entire

Disney movies word for word—especially Winnie-the-Pooh. He would become lost in this Disney world and unresponsive to any attempts to engage him or lure him into our world. During that period, he also did not sleep much at night, usually staying up playing and fussing until finally passing out asleep around four or five in the morning. Dan, who had to get up early for work, slept in Ian's racecar bed and Janet stayed up with Ian. One night when Ian was refusing to sleep but happily reciting lines from Winne-the-Pooh's The Blustery Day, Janet jumped in and took the part of Tigger: "The wonderful thing about Tiggers, is Tiggers are wonderful things! Their tops are made out of rubber! Their bottoms are made out of springs!"

Ian whipped his head around, looked her right in the eye … and burst into laughter. The joy in his smile and the relief in his eyes spoke nonverbal volumes—"Mommy, you found me!" Janet had entered Ian's world.

We embraced Ian's world. One day on television Ian discovered the world of Thomas the Tank Engine. He soon knew every train, every person, and every word of every dialogue. We bought him a train table and all the trains we could find. All. Of. Them. When we brought everything home and set it up, Ian was so excited he didn't stop playing, even to eat, for DAYS (OK, a day and a half, but it felt like FOREVER. He would occasionally fall asleep for a nap beside the train table). We became concerned and reached out for advice to therapists, behaviorists, and friends. We were told to stop him and NOT to indulge in this OBSESSION. We were told to put the trains away and make Ian focus on other things—age-appropriate things like riding a bicycle or climbing a tree.

However, we watched carefully and after that first insane day or so, Ian resumed eating and sleeping so we let it continue. His play with these toys remained intense as was the joy on our son's face, the rapture as he played out scenes from the TV series on his own Thomas track—and he started trying to talk. Ian would put the trains on the edge of a table facing each other and he would put his face right up to them and act out the interactions between characters by speaking (well, jabbering). He was telling stories. When he went to bed, he would line up the Thomas trains on his nightstand carefully so that the trains were facing each other (so they could talk to each other). It was VERY obsessive, but our son was learning about communicating. We kept the Thomas trains and we have never regretted this decision. He began to talk using more vocabulary and his overly obsessive behaviors with the trains diminished.

Ian's sleep issues (as in, he didn't sleep) eventually drove us to use medication to help him sleep. We had started to hear legends about eliminating wheat and dairy from a child's diet to reduce or "cure" autism. Dan was VERY skeptical since there was no scientific basis for this diet. But he tried it himself for a couple of days and found it made him feel dramatically better, improved his energy and ability to concentrate, and helped him to be more easygoing. We put Ian on the diet and found immediate improvement in his ability to regulate himself. His teachers reported that Ian's ability to participate in school and attend to lessons improved. He also started to have a normal sleep pattern and we were able to back off all medication.

Ian's improvement at school helped him learn to read quickly, and to support his reading we turned on the closed captions on all television programs so he could read the lines that Thomas and his friends were saying. We think this helped Ian understand that reading was really talking. He still is very good at reading aloud even when he doesn't understand all of the text. He has developed a deep connection to storytelling. He would often create a circle with his stuffed animals and read to them. He even set up a library so that his animals could check out their own books. All this at a time when his ability to communicate verbally was still very, very low. Looking at videos from this time Ian spoke in single words and had a very small vocabulary.

By entering and embracing our son's world, we leveraged other styles of communication. Connecting his imagination to the real world and to other people in his life has created a bridge between his world and ours. We use many of these techniques daily working with other students in our program at Autistry and call it "meeting them where they are."

10
LOVE IS WHY WE ARE HERE

Dawn A. Witte

I write this as a love note from my soul to yours. You are worthy, you are important, you matter, and you were born to bring something special to this world that only you can bring in a way that only you can. I believe this to be true for each and every one of us. If we do not know this about ourselves consciously, our souls know it. We just get to remember it.

Raising my daughters and a menagerie of pets filled my life with purpose and passion. I loved nurturing my daughters, Taylor and Carrington, and shepherding them into adulthood. I viewed my role as a mom very seriously and took every opportunity to be a part of everything they did. From being a classroom volunteer in their classes to coaching their soccer teams, I wanted to be an active participant in their childhood journeys. I cherished every moment, even the challenging ones. However, if we do our job well as a parent, our children will grow up to become independent adults and will not need the same type of support and nurturing they did when they were young. I was not a perfect mom, but I did raise two extraordinary young ladies who I am so blessed to have as daughters.

When my girls were in college, I started looking at my own life and asking myself what the next chapter of my life would be. I had no idea what that was because I had not thought about my life independently of them. One day I was sitting in my favorite spot outside and asked God, my angels, my dad, who had passed away in 2000, "What am I even good at?"

I had spent so many years cooking, cleaning, volunteering, and taking care of everyone that I did not see any value in myself outside of what I could do for my family. The answer that came to me very clearly and concisely was, "You know how to love people well."

My first thought was, "What the heck do I do with that?" It was not an answer that gave me any type of clarity and I put it out of my mind, temporarily, while I went back to cleaning, cooking, and running errands like I had before, but I was still feeling a call to something more.

Still in search for the more I was seeking, I took courses and earned certifications. I attended conferences and started on a journey of personal discovery that would begin unfolding more and more each day. In November of 2016 I attended a Glamour Women's Conference in Hollywood, California. During a mixer at the end of the day's events I saw a beautiful woman wearing a very pretty long white dress and a stunning gold necklace. She was absolutely gorgeous and because I believe that when you see something beautiful in someone you should let them know, I walked up to her and told her how beautiful her outfit was. She thanked me and told me that her outfit was from her country, Ghana. She continued to tell me that she was going to be crowned queen of her village the following April and I told her that I had always wanted to visit Africa. She told me that I should come. That conversation sparked a series of events that would change my life forever.

When I got home from the conference, I looked online for information about Ghana and volunteer opportunities in schools or orphanages. I knew I had always wanted to go to Africa to visit children. The ones I had read and heard about my whole life.

Children who did not have parents or were living in poverty. That was always something that had been placed upon my heart, but until meeting that beautiful woman, I had never thought about doing anything about that calling. I found a volunteer opportunity and signed up to try to align my dates with the Queen's coronation.

At that time, I was working with Laura Swan, an amazing transformational coach. A few weeks before I embarked on my trip, Laura guided me through a meditation and asked what I envisioned for my trip. I am not great at meditating, but Laura was always able to get me to a place where I could tap into the visions of my soul.

Laura asked me questions about what I wanted to see and do while I was in Africa. Truthfully, I wanted to go and meet the children I had seen in my dreams. The ones who had been orphaned and struggled to get enough food or basic necessities. I wanted to let them know they were loved and that I loved them even though I had never met them. I loved them because they existed. That is what I did know. As she was guiding me through the meditation, I had a picture of beautiful African children wearing school uniforms and, in my mind, I thought, "Well of course you got that picture in your mind because that is what you are going there for."

The next image that came to me was that of a brown wall on a dirt road. The skeptic in me was thinking, "You have seen pictures like this before so of course these are the images that you are seeing." The next image that came to me was a grey wall with a PVC pipe that was cut flush with the wall. Now that vision stumped me because I had no idea where that came from. Laura said, "Maybe you are going to bring water to them." I wasn't thinking about bringing water to anyone. I was going to meet and love the children I had dreamed about my whole life.

A few weeks later I traveled to Africa on a trip that would change my life for the best forever. I was looking for that wall and I was looking for that PVC pipe because I wanted to see if that vision held some message for me.

When I arrived at the school/orphanage in Ghana where I signed up to volunteer, I was so happy. The volunteers had daily assignments and we would wake up early in the morning to help the children bathe and get ready for school. After the children started school, we would help serve them breakfast from giant black kettles and deliver the meals to each classroom. After breakfast, the volunteers had a break to do whatever we wanted before it was time to help serve and deliver the lunches. I would take that time to go to the preschool room where there were children ranging from babies to five years old. I absolutely loved visiting them because they were so happy to have someone there who absolutely loved and adored them.

On the second or third day visiting the classroom, with children surrounding me, I looked up to see a window and out of that window I saw that same vision of a grey wall with a PVC pipe, cut flush. I had chills throughout my body because I saw in the physical world what I had only seen in the vision I had weeks before. That was a moment I will never forget. I took a picture of it because I never want to forget seeing that image.

Upon returning home, I finished my life coaching certification and embarked on my second trip to Africa. This time, going to Ghana was not enough. I added Uganda, Kenya, and Rwanda to my itinerary. While we were driving through the villages, I was seeing the poverty and the lack. I had just finished being taught that we live in an abundant universe and that if we ask God for help, he will provide. I was trying to reconcile that notion with what I was seeing in the lives of the people I was surrounded by. I could not make sense of it until it came to me that maybe I was an answer to that mother's prayer. Maybe somehow, God let me hear her prayer and that is why I was called to do the work I do. Again, it hit me, we are here to do God's work here on this earth. We are all here to answer someone's prayers and someone else is here to be an answer to ours.

Fast forward several years and I have spent over four months in Africa, traveling to six different countries and meeting thousands of children. My life has been transformed because I said yes to a dream, which I held in my heart for nearly my entire life. I do not know why I felt so called to go to Africa. Many of the countries I have traveled to were because I trusted the Universe and I followed my soul's calling. I had no guarantee that things would turn out the way they have and that I would have found a calling and purpose greater than anything I could have even imagined but I followed my faith and I listened to my soul.

We did indeed drill a borehole at the Savior Children's Foundation to bring clean water to the children who live and go to school there. In addition to that borehole, we have also drilled two other boreholes in Ghana, bringing water to communities that needed it. We also built a medical bay in a community that had no medical facilities near them. We have moved our children in Sierra Leone from a one-room dwelling where all the children slept on the floor to a home where they all have beds. We have done a major wharf cleanup, created classes and enrichment programs for our children in Ghana, and met basic needs for our children in Uganda for the past five years. We have personally delivered nearly 2,500 copies of The Little Books of Be … to children in Rwanda, Kenya, Uganda, Sierra Leone, and Ghana. And I know this is just the beginning of the work that I will continue to do on the continent of Africa and beyond.

The only way I can explain that vision of that PVC pipe in that wall is from something greater than what I can explain in terms of our physical existence alone. I was given that image because God already knew what he called me to do here on this earth. I am so grateful that I listened to my heart and my soul when I embarked on the unknown because my life is much better for it. I get to live in the knowledge that there are children around the world who have breathed easier because I have existed, and I believe that is what we are all here to do.

Reflecting on that day sitting outside where I received the message, "You know how to love people well," I now understand that love is the best thing we can be good at. Love is our highest and greatest currency, and I am so grateful and happy that I followed that message because it has led me on the greatest journey. By stepping out into the unknown, I found a renewed purpose and passion for life. I understand my worth and the value I bring to this world. We all have value and something to bring to this world and we can achieve extraordinary things when we BELIEVE.

11

THE LUCKY ONES

Ndidi Rickert

My sister, brother, and I stood frozen at Charles de Gaulle Airport. It was 1991 and Dad had worked to receive three free airline tickets with Union de Transports Aériens (UTA) for us to go to Sierra Leone on vacation from England where we were attending school.

"Oh my God! Where are the passports?" Ngozi said.

"What do you mean? You had all three of them in your passport holder thingy," I replied.

"I don't know where they are. I may have misplaced them. Oh my God! The last time I remember having them was in the cab," Ngozi cried.

"What do you mean?" I was distraught. "You never lose anything. Deary me. Our flight is in less than two hours!"

We ran back to where the taxi driver had dropped us off, where we were to catch a flight to Sierra Leone. When we left Dover for Calais, it had been fun, but in Paris it was one thing after another. First, Nnamdi had suffered a slight bout of food poisoning. Then there was a transit strike, which delayed us even further.

We may have stood there for twenty nail-biting minutes when we saw a car that looked like the one that just dropped us off, driving toward us. It was him! The same driver! Same blue shirt. He jumped out and handed the passport holder to us, speaking in French explaining that when he saw the black holder in the back seat, he knew he had to come back to us.

We were elated. With utter disbelief, he restored our faith in humanity. Finally, something was going right. I could've hugged him.

"Merci, Merci beaucoup, mille merci," Ngozi said.

"Tres bien, Merci infiniment," I chimed.

We checked that all three passports were intact and we were so grateful. We looked at each other and bolted for the ticket counter where we checked in, ran through to the gates, and there we were all ready to board. We were going to make it after all.

The flight from France to Freetown, Sierra Leone, felt longer than usual. I was certain it felt that long because we were excited to see Daddy and our friends. We were lucky again to have been surprised by Daddy. As he had always done, he negotiated tickets for his three children from one of his jobs with UTA Airlines.

After many hours and an awfully long and boring flight, the plane landed at Lungi Airport. We were home. "Land that we love, our Sierra Leone." When the airplane doors opened in Freetown, something inside of me screamed with joy.

"We're home. Can you believe it?" I said as we walked down the stairs disembarking from the plane to the tarmac.

The air was warm, balmy, and beautiful. Hearing the chaos, the cries, and the confusion, I knew I was home. One does not arrive in Freetown without the quintessential chaos, the cries of people greeting their relatives, and the confusions staged by pick-pocketers and "raray man dem" (translation: young men who have no jobs) all waiting to harass the Johnny-Just-Comes (JJCs). An envoy of us had landed and The Serry-Kamal, The Eccles-James, and The Beckley-Lines families were together once again.

Eki, my favorite cousin, was there to meet us at the airport. "Let's get the party started," he said.

Typically, arriving at Lungi airport was only one step of the way. We then had to cross over a ferry into Freetown. Depending on the times, there were always a variety of ways to get to mainland Freetown. One could either take the speedboat, the helicopter, the ferry, or drive. Irrespective of how you sliced it, it was a long and sometimes the most treacherous leg of the way.

Paying homage to the beach was a ritual. Even before heading home, we would head straight to the beach for a meal at a beach bar, drink, and listen to music as the waves crashed in the background. How we typically spent our first hours back was to spend time together until the wee hours and then go home to crash, or our group of friends would herd us to a nightclub to dance the night away before returning to the beach to watch the sunrise. For many expatriate friends, this was the holy grail. It blew their minds. For us who grew up here, it was just another Wednesday.

While on holiday in Freetown, we were on a mission. During the day, we visited with aunts and uncles, as is customary. At night, we partied like it was 1999.

One crazy evening, we left home for Lagoonda, the destination nightclub at the time, then left for the first party of the night, where we partied until five in the morning. We then stopped off at Paddy's Beach Bar, my favorite. At this time of the night, the only thing left at Paddy's were the hideous leftover Kolonkos (prostitutes), whom even the drunkest white men did not want.

We refused to disband and go home so someone suggested we head to theirs. A bunch of us descended on Arina and Eki's home. They were our cousins who lived on Spur Road. We were eating breakfast when the news was interrupted by a strange local alarm over the radio.

"Attention, attention, this is not a drill. We are informing you there has been a coup d'état. You need to stay wherever you are. There will be a three-day curfew. No one should be on the streets."

"What? Is this real?" Ngozi asked. At this point most were leaning on each other, starting to fall asleep, a couple of people were still eating and a couple were making out in the corner.

"Oh, oh, that doesn't sound good," I said.

"We can continue the party," one of us said. "I don't want to go home anyway."

"Did you not hear them? They said we were to stay put wherever we are for three days."

Indeed, we stayed at the Eccles-James' for three days; with the same clothes we had worn to the nightclub three days before.

On the second day, two trucks pulled up in front of their gate, honking their horns. Afraid, we scurried around wanting to hide, knowing they would find us anyway. We begged the gatekeeper not to open the gate, but he couldn't refuse. We knew they could shoot him and us without any repercussions. We had heard of soldiers taking a lot of drugs, and as such, acting senselessly. Dad had told us of reports of soldiers opening bullets and mixing gunpowder with cocaine to make them even more fierce.

The Land Rover Wolf entered the compound. An identical one followed right behind. Each had eight to ten soldiers hanging on to the back, side, and front of the vehicle. They exhibited frightening bravado, each with his personalized AK-47 rifle slung across his body.

"Kushe oh, Mr. Eric, what do you have for us?" one of them asked, reeking of alcohol. They jumped out of the vehicle and dispersed in and around the house and the compound. Some were smoking cigarettes, one was smoking marijuana, and a couple went upstairs. The way they looked at us was scary. There was nothing any of us could do.

"Nothing, staying home, trying to protect the children," Uncle Eric said.

"Where is your G-Class?" one of them asked.

"It's been giving me problems. It's been in the garage for a while now, still waiting for the parts," Uncle Eric replied.

"You got any dollars?" they asked him.

"Not on me but I can give you guys everything I have right now."

Uncle removed wads of clean, crisp notes from his pocket. He handed them over to the boss soldier.

"You are di man. Correct!" Boss soldier looked at the wad of money, trying to estimate how much he had just been given. He whistled at the others.

"Let's go!" He banged the Land Rover hood with his gun. One of them snatched Uncle Eric's sunglasses and jumped into the back of the vehicle. The rest of the soldiers in the compound jumped back in and on the side of the vehicle, none of them sitting down. They left, promising to be back.

We were gobsmacked yet relieved. We watched in horror at the lawlessness of what was going on.

On the third day, my Dad walked from Tengbeh Town to Spur Road to be with his children. We convinced him we were fine, so he left. We assured him there was nothing to be afraid of.

It was a beautiful morning and conflicting in all the ways possible because what was happening was anything but. The air was tense. The soldiers were curt. No one knew where President Major General Joseph Saidu Momoh had fled and the soldiers who took over were ruthless. There were stories of the atrocities they were performing, unleashing terror every chance they got.

In the evening, we asked the driver to drop us off at Nana's home where we were staying. This ride from Spur Road to Juba Hill was stressful, long, and eerie, like something out of a movie. Men in combat fatigues swarmed the streets in army vehicles, with guns everywhere. There were hardly any people on the streets. It seemed like every few yards there were soldiers swarming barricades, and we were stopped several times on our short ride. The daytime curfew had been lifted but people were too afraid to leave their houses. At night, there were stories of looting.

Finally, we got to my friend Nana's place and were able to call Mummy.

"Things have been so tough for such a long time, it's no wonder there was a coup," Mum said. She was relieved we were all together and sounding surprisingly chirpy. "People are tired of suffering," she said.

The following day we were reprimanded by another set of soldiers with guns when, while staying at Juba Hill and being a bunch of bored teenagers, we came up with the idea of hiking up to Pa Sheki's house to see what they'd done to it. This was the ex-president's house.

On our way there, to our shock and dismay, we passed Mr. Abdulai Conteh's house. It had been viciously looted. We were friends with his children, and we'd been to the house many times for birthday parties. It felt so sad.

Soon we opened the gates to Pa Sheki's. His massive pool was there, glistening, beckoning us to take a quick plunge when suddenly, a bunch of soldiers showed up. They had us all kneel with our faces against the wall. This time, they were not laughing. After a few threats, a few of us started crying and begging, scared of what these soldiers might do next. I can't remember what we did but they finally escorted us out of the gates and off we went.

We laughed about it when we got home but that insane outing shook us to our core. Anything could have happened. We were busy spending cherished moments with childhood friends being ridiculous, but this was no time for that. We were at war.

Not long after, the airlines started canceling flights. It was considered a full-on conflict and as such liability was too high. On the news, we could hear that the Americans had evacuated all US citizens and warned against anyone staying in Sierra Leone. My father wanted us out of there.

Soon, we learned that a chartered jumbo jet was being sent to evacuate the Germans. We also learned that if there was space, people with European passports would be next in line. My Dad called the British consulate and put our names on the list.

"No, Daddy, we're not done with our vacation yet," I protested. We had only just arrived.

"Daddy, will you come with us?" Nnamdi asked.

"No," Dad said, "I'll hold the fort here until things blow over."

Regrettably, they didn't just blow over. It was going to be a long time before we saw our father again and many more years before we saw some of our friends.

The German airplane arrived, and Dad had arranged everything. All I kept thinking of was that I hadn't said goodbye to my friends. Suddenly, we were throwing everything in our suitcases again, grabbing our toiletries from the bathroom and Dad was waiting to drive us to the helipad. Sanira and another friend were at the helipad waiting to say goodbye to us. We hugged Daddy and our friends and wept as we walked to the helicopter.

In an effort to savor my last memories of Freetown, I looked back and the sight was heartbreaking. Swarms of police were everywhere. I turned to look at my friends once more when it dawned on me—goodness me, we were at war. Again, it felt like I was watching a movie, only this time, we were the actors. No, we were not acting, this was real life. We boarded the helicopter and were transported to the airport.

At the airport, we stood behind a small family. They had been waiting eagerly to be allowed to travel together. The family consisted of a white man, probably an expatriate whom none of us could recognize, and a black Sierra Leonean woman, who was evidently the mother of their mixed-race toddler. Waiting patiently behind them, we could feel their nervousness. One soldier announced the gentleman's name as well as what seemed like his son's name. All three of them walked up to the gate begging for the mother to be allowed on the plane so they all would be together as one family.

"No sir, she cannot get on that plane," one soldier told them.

To convince the soldier, the gentleman went on to explain that he had called the head of the British High Commission prior, who told them that if there was space on the plane, his partner would be allowed to travel with them.

"My friend, I don't care if you called Jesus, if this woman is not an EU citizen, we cannot let her on the plane," the soldier repeated.

They instructed the gentleman and his toddler to get on the plane. The poor little boy clung to his mother for dear life. He was weeping as they pulled him away from his mum. I can still hear the shrill of his voice. The lady stood there sobbing deeply. It was painful to watch. I wonder sometimes what happened to her and if she was ever reunited with her family.

We gave the tightest hugs to our father, boarded the plane, and were silent. This had been an ordeal. I distinctly remember feeling blessed enough to have had a second passport. We recognized our privilege and were ridden with guilt that there were others out there who wanted to escape the brutality of war but couldn't. What had become of our Sierra Leone? What had we witnessed? When would we see Daddy again?

We boarded the jumbo jet and sadly noticed after settling into our seats, that the plane wasn't even full. Heartbreaking.

The resulting civil would go on to last for ten years, nine months, three weeks, and five days, consuming the country and though exact numbers may never be known, it has been estimated that the civil war claimed over fifty thousand lives in Sierra Leone. Sadly, half of the Revolutionary United Front, a rebel group's army, and a quarter of the government armed forces consisted of children aged eight to fourteen years old.

We returned to England, unable to see Daddy for several years. And yet, we were the lucky ones. Despite our privilege and status, we were deeply affected by the war. When we went West, things went south, I explained it to my second-year college roommate. We may be living in a strange land, I told her, but we in the West are truly the lucky ones.

12

NEW CITY, NEW ME

Sanika Bhurke

"I've come a long way," I said to my husband, holding his hand in mine as we walked along the waterfront of San Francisco, California.

Two years before, I was single, living in this exact city, walking on this exact pathway, feeling stuck, miserable, and ready for a change. Like many, I worked in the technology industry of Silicon Valley. I had a great job, a beautiful apartment with views of the water, and many wonderful opportunities to learn, grow, and meet smart, accomplished people. I may have appeared to be successful on the outside, but inside, I was unfulfilled. Little did I know that my life in this city was at the precipice of a fundamental shift waiting to happen.

I woke up one day feeling in my bones that it was time for a change. After years of doing the inner work, I finally had the courage to listen to my inner voice. As someone who was immersed in the culture of Silicon Valley at the peak of my career, I chose to believe that there was more to life. I made the brave choice, to move sight unseen, in the middle of the pandemic, to a new city in a new country.

When I landed in Vancouver, British Columbia, on the eve of my thirties, the first of my two affirmations went like this: "This is the first day of the rest of my life." I was determined to keep moving forward, change the course of my life, get in touch with myself, and be genuinely peaceful and happy.

I was also ready to meet the love of my life. Hence, my second affirmation: "Men in Vancouver are amazing." I convinced myself with my self-talk, "I'm simply walking toward all that my heart desires. It's all done and set up for me. I am open to receiving my glorious new life and my future husband."

The path to listening to myself, embracing my inner world, and trusting my voice hasn't come easy. The beginning of my journey of transformation has roots in Chicago, Illinois. I was in my early twenties, and I had freshly graduated from Indiana University Bloomington with a master's degree. I had converted my summer internship to a full-time job offer in Chicago, and I was ready, energetic, and eager to start my career in Big Four consulting. Lyrics to Kelly Clarkson's song came alive every time I badged in through the office doors overlooking scenic views of Chicago's skyline and Lake Michigan.

Buildings with a hundred floors,
Swinging round revolving doors,
Maybe I don't know where they'll take me, but
Gotta keep moving on, moving on, fly away, breakaway …

I hit a breaking point somewhere along this journey of flying high in my career. I found myself easily startled and shaking in work meetings. The nights were worse. I couldn't fall asleep with racing thoughts in my head, and I woke up with butterflies in my stomach. There were moments when everything felt way too much, as if my whole world was going to crash any minute. I gathered the courage and signed on to work on managing my recurring feelings of anxiety and overwhelm. As I continued on this journey, I found various practices to help me manage my life. Slowly but surely, as I got better, this became a journey of self-discovery and self-awareness.

What started as a reaction to a breakdown became a proactive approach to finding my sense of self. Knowing that I have made it through every single one of my tough days has given me the confidence and resilience to navigate life's challenges with grace. I am more accepting of our human condition, breaking away from perfectionism, and have an elevated sense of compassion for the world around and within me.

I grew up in a city close to Mumbai, India, always dreaming of studying and living abroad. The world of my childhood was a safe bubble. I went to school, went to tuitions, met friends and family, and did the same routine all over again the next day. Everything revolved around getting good grades as is very typical of life in India in the '90s. I did manage to sneak in a lot of extracurricular activities and have fun. At the same time, I was curious and eager to explore the bigger world around me.

I had a deep sense of wonder. I read and pretended to teach invisible students, in my make-believe childhood world, the Childcraft book series, sort of an encyclopedia for young children, of which I had all fifteen volumes. I loved Archie comics, which gave a glimpse of teenage life in America, and Tintin comics where they traveled all over the world solving mysteries. When my close relatives visited from the United States during the summer, bearing gifts such as Chapstick or an Oral-B toothbrush, I was fascinated by their stories. It was a small glimpse into life outside of my safe bubble in India.

Of course, this was back in the dawn of the twenty-first century when avenues for understanding the world beyond where you lived were far fewer than in today's world of YouTube and global brands. I sometimes wonder what created the fascination for going abroad but it's always been there. My first trip abroad was to New York City when I was nineteen. I felt like I was in a movie, standing in the middle of Times Square, with big billboards above, and the yellow taxi cabs around me. After a missed opportunity to study abroad for my undergraduate degree in Singapore, which led to a series of events leading to meeting my fiancé, I got my chance to finally move abroad. I was sitting on a plane to study in the United States of America for a graduate degree. I was so excited! I packed my entire childhood into a couple of suitcases and off I went.

Over time, I've packed my life in boxes and suitcases many times in pursuit of my dreams. My move from Chicago to San Francisco was the beginning of my purging, shedding of old skin, and making way for a new me. I was hoping that my move to California would be "it." After a rough period of anxiety and panic in Chicago, all I wanted was to find a sense of grounding and peace with my move to San Francisco.

Instead of grounding, I found myself up in the air, flying every month between San Francisco and Chicago to complete a leadership coach training program. However much I tried to find my ground in the city, I always found myself up in the air. I was like a plant refusing to take root in the soil that I found under my feet.

I didn't know back then that I was still in the middle of it—the middle of my transformation. Chicago was the beginning, San Francisco was the middle … and there was another leg to go. This was a journey with multiple stops. With every move came a loss of what was, to make room for the creation of what my future was calling me to be. Loss is painful and losing my old self felt unbearable at times. It came with this sense of leaving people and places behind that I couldn't take forward on my journey. With every loss, I was creating space to inch closer to the new me.

I think to myself, the longest flight I have taken is possibly from Mumbai to Chicago. However, the few years I spent in San Francisco, in the middle of the pandemic, taking flight from my old self to gently growing and nurturing my new self, that journey has felt the longest. I also think that in hindsight I am glad I had the naivety and the curiosity to explore the world, as that led to the biggest journey, which has been to explore the depths of my inner world.

I like to call Vancouver the last leg of my transformation journey. When I landed here, I had tears in my eyes and this deep sense of knowing in my body. I am home. I was right. I had found my place in the world. The clues stacked up. I found my permanent apartment in the same building that I was Airbnb-ing in. I had accepted a job offer that I was excited about. And the best of it all? I met my partner, my now-fiancé, three weeks into moving to Vancouver, who coincidentally lived two blocks away from me. I was watching my affirmation come to life.

My whole world was set up for me, and I was simply walking into it open to receive the gifts of the Universe. To sum it up, I not only moved to a new city, but also a whole new country, started an exciting new job, met my life partner, and most importantly, found myself and my peace of mind. Possibly for the first time in my life, at the age of twenty-nine, I felt connected to a deep and genuine happiness within me.

I know that I am a new person, the person I was striving to be when I first started my journey in Chicago. She is here. I am her now. I am no longer reaching and searching for her. I am her. Every single day of my life. I love being her. She is present, peaceful, happy, loving, and joyful. She made it through the tough times! I am so happy for her. I am grateful and I feel blessed. All the letters I wrote to the Universe when I was in a hard place asking to be in a better place … it turns out, the Universe was listening. All the efforting, all the work … was worth it. Thank you, Universe.

13

A GIFT OF TIME

Janae Hunderman

The year 2020 was the best year of my life. I said it. It can be hard to claim your own thriving in the midst of others' worst struggles. It took a long time to be able to own this powerful year for myself and even longer to be able to say it aloud.

Before the pandemic, I had been having a challenging time. It is not one of those rock-bottom wake-up-on-the-bathroom-floor-and-realize-your-life-is-a-mess kind of stories with a sensational comeback, rather everything just felt a little … off. I had a steady relationship, a steady job, good friendships, a loving family, and affordable rent in a desirable community. I had it all but felt just …fine.

I had been with my boyfriend for a couple of years, and he was clearly an amazing human and the right person for me, but not yet in that partnership way that I was hoping for. However great on the cover, I wasn't sure we were on the same page in life, or maybe not even in the same book. I'm a bookworm and he doesn't read, what was I expecting, right? I had higher hopes, but there was nothing wrong that I could put my finger on. Maybe this was as good as it gets.

My health was just OK as well. I had been living with chronic pain that was, at times, so debilitating that it got in the way of enjoying friendships or getting outside into the natural beauty I was lucky enough to be surrounded by. After years of trying to find answers, and even becoming a certified health coach, I wondered if this was as good as it could get.

The work I was doing was impactful, fulfilling, and made a difference. But as someone who loves learning and growing, there was no career ladder in sight. Equally important, the work environment was anything but healthy. I basked in the glorious life-changing impact my work was having, only to be thwacked on the side of the head by colleagues' stress and drama; the roller coaster of success and distress was wearing on me, but maybe this was as good as it gets.

In 2018, I had received a forwarded mass email with an opportunity. I completely disregarded it. Shortly after, I received the same forwarded mass email, this time from someone I knew and respected. I completely disregarded it. But the opportunity nagged me, an uninvited guest popping into my head a few times a day. I applied at the last minute and was accepted.

I then found myself in a yearlong training, driving hundreds of miles every month to spend a weekend with strangers talking about things like career development, teamwork, and emotional intelligence. Emotional intelligence with a bunch of strangers, as if that would work.

Then the emotional intelligence segment was queued up. Before the leadership coach even spoke, I knew I wanted to be her. I was surrounded by others' stress at work yet she got to talk about mindsets, perspectives, and feelings for a living. We were lucky to have one-on-one coaching sessions with her every month, but I was especially enthralled with the idea that she was having these deep, life-altering conversations with each of us. In our third month, she announced that we'd be discussing coaching skills from Co-Active Coaching, Fourth Edition: The Proven Framework for

Transformative Conversations in Work and in Life by Henry Kimsey-House, Karen Kimsey-House, Phillip Sandahl and Laura Whitworth. Maybe my life wasn't as good as it gets? I bought the book online before she even started her presentation. The book's discount code inspired me to sign up for the initial Co-Active Fundamentals course shortly after with a noncommittal sort of curiosity.

And then, cancer arrived in my world in the summer of 2019. When your dad calls you to tell you that he has cancer and the solution is to remove an entire organ from his body, you begin to see things a little differently. My dad's sister had recently been going through her own battle, but before that, the C-word had always been someone else's story, one that my family had seemingly dodged for generations.

Faced with the very real potential of not having my dad cheering me along, I wondered what my impact was meant to be. My dad had always been a mentor to others, and with the possibility that he might not be around much longer, I knew my work was to embrace the skills that I had inherited from him. No longer willing to accept "as good as it gets," I dove headfirst into becoming a coach and signed up for the entire series of Co-Active coursework rather than just the Fundamentals course. I started my LLC, opened a business bank account, and offered my first coaching session outside my dad's hospital room.

After completing the initial coursework, I began certification in the second week of March of 2020. When I attended my first virtual certification cohort meeting, I knew these were my people, each of these budding coaches was equally committed to a demanding training and acquiring top-notch skills and credentials. I knew our lives were going to change in our time together, little did I know how much.

The week my certification began, I was simultaneously leading an artist retreat for a group of high school teenagers in Ghost Ranch, New Mexico. I knew some strange things were happening in the world—my flight to Europe for spring break had been canceled due to this strange virus—but I was disconnected from the news while surrounded by the inspiration of blossoming young artists in the desert of Georgia O'Keefe.

When a volunteer parent arrived, she verified what I couldn't believe from the bits of news I'd followed; there really was no toilet paper in the stores at home. That Friday, as I drove the fourteen-passenger school bus full of tired teenagers, I had a sense that our lives would change forever the moment they stepped off those ridged gray steps. Before pulling the big magical lever that both opens the door and puts out a flashing stop sign, I shared the smallest bit of wisdom I could muster: "Everyone is going to experience different emotions, and that's OK. Let yourself feel what you need to feel." I was already a coach.

Even with a coach's mindset, I didn't realize how much life could improve during a worldwide pandemic. It's so cliché, it's painful. It's so true, I can't avoid saying it: coaching changed my life.

Luckily for me, coach certification was already set up to be virtual, so we were able to continue without a hitch. Coach training involves learning new concepts in a class setting, reading about those concepts, practicing those concepts with other coaches, getting feedback on your coaching from peer coaches and master coaches, and having your own coach. In short, you're completely immersed in a coaching way of being, you are consistently receiving coaching, and you have a team of coaches cheering you along.

With more time around the apartment, my partner and I had committed to a healthier lifestyle including cleaning up our diets, getting more exercise, and connecting on regular walks together. While traipsing down the hillside of a nearby hike, I casually started asking some coaching questions. "What do you hope your life will look like in eight years? In five years? In three years?" I shared my own dreams in response. We were struck by the clear alignment in our goals. We both had a desire to create a home, preferably with a little space and a garden. We could picture the impact of our careers growing in ways that didn't make sense yet felt possible. We both wanted healthy bodies, minds, and hearts. We were a perfect match. We could see it clearly and our gratitude for each other has only grown since then.

Work was still a roller coaster, albeit from a virtual distance. Visions of a larger career impact had come in multiple ways and for the first time, I started to truly believe I was meant for more impact and a wider reach. I'm from a small town where the opportunities to do the kind of work I was doing seemed limited. Then my ideas collided with the confidence my coach was helping me gain, and I was able to create a new job opportunity for myself mid-pandemic. A year and a half later, that opportunity opened the door to another one, and then another one after that. I'll spare you the résumé recital, but I went from thinking coaching was the only option forward, to having coaching propel my career forward and uncovering options previously unimaginable.

Meanwhile, my partner and I continued to talk about our dreams, and that future home became a recurring theme. Out of town versus in town? Build from the ground up or remodel something fun and funky? Financially, we couldn't imagine how an educator and musician were going to make it work so the dream felt fun but distant. Then my realtor friend randomly called to check in on our pandemic lives. I answered with, "The irony is, of course, it's you who calls while I'm scrolling Zillow." Being a fantastic professional, she asked what I was looking at. When I told her, she shared that a particular piece of vacant land was really special, and we should look at it. So, we did. And it was. And we found a way to buy it. The point isn't how we did it, the point is that if we hadn't been considering what we wanted to create, we wouldn't have recognized the opportunity when it arrived. Some call it manifestation, others say it's answered prayers. I say that believing that this doesn't have to be as good as it gets can open your eyes and create your 2020 vision.

Through coaching, I learned to dream big and listen to the small voice of wisdom inside myself. I gained clarity on what I want to offer the world. I learned to love myself a little more. Because of this, I ended 2020 with a healthier relationship, a healthier body, an inspiring career trajectory, as a landowner, and as a certified coach with a growing business. Like any story, there are pieces I left out, parts in the wrong order, likely a little exaggeration here and there. In my coaching practice, I often start by reviewing all aspects of a client's life situation before digging into the main topic, and it is no exaggeration to say that my entire life improved dramatically: relationships, career, health, friendships, family, finances, personal growth, level of impact and more.

Life is still a work in progress. My partner still fascinates me and is my best playground for personal growth. Our dream house is under construction, and like life, it's a painfully delicious process. My dad is healthy, and we continue to marvel at how much we have in common. My professional life is rich and varied, I'm enjoying navigating and embracing the multitude of opportunities as they arise or are intentionally created. My clients never cease to inspire me, and my coaches and coach friends hold a mirror up for me to realign my visions for clarity and then to realign again and again.

I'm becoming comfortable with never fully arriving, and the journey is so beautiful.

We wore flashing neon glasses to celebrate New Year's Eve in 2019; we hoped the fresh 2020 vision was going to bring us the best year yet. The vision was not what we expected, yet I'm thankful for the journey. My eyes are more open and I'm forever grateful for the beauty of that year of growth.

14

DEATH AND TRANSFIGURATION

Susan Drury

In 1989, I was a thirty-one-year-old wife, mother, and part-time singer/actress, living a seemingly normal life. Suddenly out of the blue, I began experiencing excruciating shooting, burning pain in the side of my face. Although this appeared to be random with no explanation (no recent dental work, traumatic accident, or brain tumor), I was going through a very distressing time in my life and the entrapment within terrible pain was an apt metaphor for the helplessness I was feeling in my outer circumstances.

Eventually diagnosed with trigeminal neuralgia, I began exploring everything conventional medicine could offer to ameliorate this condition, but each time was returned yet again into the grips of pain. Ultimately it occurred to me that this was a mystery only I could solve—and so began my personal and then professional journey into the transformational healing arts, for myself, and for others.

Over these past thirty-some years, my life has been one of gradual expansion and thriving on so many levels—however severe, physical pain has continued to be a companion that I am regularly forced to respect. While we all might wish pain would cease to exist, for now, it seems to remain an inevitable part of the human journey—and may even become an unexpected pathway into a more expansive state of being. I share with you a recent experience where pain became my catalyst for transfiguration and new freedom.

It had been a challenging few months. The neuralgia had suddenly ramped up—and up and up—shortly after the New Year. I resisted taking the pharmaceutical drugs for a while, but after many difficult nights of constantly interrupted sleep and days where I could barely eat or talk without triggering the knifing pain, reluctantly I gave in.

Starting up with these anticonvulsants is a slippery slope, as they have become less effective over the years, and the rebound of pain as the medication wears off is even more heightened. Going on them means a gradual ramping up in dosage over weeks or months before the episode finally starts to wane. Only then can I slowly decrease the dosage over some weeks. Once the pain is less frequent and tolerable, they can finally be stopped completely.

I had recently gone through that cycle, and was blessedly off the drugs, with much less daily pain. There had, however, been another very disturbing happening several times over the past months—sudden severe chest/shoulder/neck pain—which had sent me to the emergency room three separate times. Mysteriously, no abnormality was ever found, so I was sent home with an apologetic shrug, and over the next few weeks, the pain would slowly disappear.

It had been a couple of months since that last trip to the hospital, but I remained hyperaware of my whole body, attuned to whatever processes were taking place within it. Although the months had been difficult, part of me was holding this as some kind of physiological transfiguration: a revolution or sea change at the most basic level of my cellular structure. And now it seemed as though a corner had been turned, and I was surfacing into a more stable physical experience. Until one night.

During the evening, unprovoked, the trigeminal pain in my face had become slightly reactivated—but I went to bed without any great trepidation. Although my mind was alerted to the sudden upsurge, I consciously chose not to trigger any alarms and instead remain neutral to the sensations.

I settled myself into bed and closed my eyes, readying to sleep. Vaguely aware of my husband, Dennis, coming out of the bathroom and climbing into his side of the bed. Just another normal, perfectly fine, night.

Until … the tingling began around my left jaw. I registered the awareness, still unperturbed, still somewhat distanced. But then the stabbing pain suddenly, violently escalated up … the lightening jabs knifing across my cheek, the tensed explosions of pain like fireworks shooting not just across the left side of my face but throughout my entire body—which began writhing in full-on agony. Gone was my distant neutrality; I was fully immersed into excruciating, unspeakable pain. Automatically I began opening my mouth to pant in an attempt to ease, to interrupt, to somehow survive the agony as animal-like sounds were pushed out of me—and then, when I felt I could take no more, suddenly everything instantly disappeared. Gone. Zero.

Still reeling from the emotional aftershock but giddy with relief, I resettled. A few minutes later, maybe one, maybe five, the telltale tingling once again began. The cycle: building, shooting, stabbing, writhing, gasping, panting, sounding, and then disappearing once again. Total absence of pain, total relief, and rest. Until it started up, all over again.

For hours it continued. Aware that my sounds were likely disturbing Dennis and finally unable to stay in bed any longer, I stood up to take myself somewhere private for whatever would happen next. Standing up, though, triggered the most extreme, blinding pain not just in the left side of my face, but in my eyes, my head, the whole front of my face, almost dropping me to my knees. I stood with tears pouring from my eyes and snot from my nose, alternately holding my breath and then puffing it out of my mouth; making death-rattle-like sounds as the pain absorbed every single molecule of my experience, consuming all of me.

And then, again, gone.

Shakily I grabbed my bathrobe, found my slippers, and made my way downstairs to my office and my meditation chair. Whatever this process was, there was no escaping it: no bypass, just its inevitable progression into the unknown. And indeed, all too soon, the familiar wave began to build and build and shatter me into fragments yet again.

As I continued to go through the endless repetition of these cycles, I realized that I was dying. Literally. Or maybe just figuratively, it didn't really make a difference. Although the cycles of agony harkened to the contractions of giving birth, this was the blazing triumph of death's infernal fire. Having its complete way with me. The annihilation of any sense of security or selfhood, within this physical body. The me I related to as Susan was being consumed.

Burning within the flames, I lived my death. Its face was my face. Fear and pain meshed absolutely, inexorably, with no escape. Again and again the panting, the noises, the writhing as the death process continued. There was no sense of time, of space, of anything other than the endless cycles stripping me apart in torment.

But then somewhere, somehow, a shard of consciousness began to come forward. As the tides of fear would arise—of the pain, of the death—I began to perceive a tiny glimmer of something else. Of some kind of junction. A different possibility. A choice point began coalescing into awareness.

Within the burning ravages of my experience, two paths came into view. There was the familiar descent into horrified fear and eternal helplessness—or, by a slight turn, the call of a different possibility, an alternate choice. To choose to know, even within this pain, the presence of light. Ephemeral, I felt the offering opening to me. One tiny instant at a time, I disengaged from fear within this death process, and turned toward light. Toward love. Bit by bit, every single speck, every atom and molecule of my experience, no matter how tormented, I deliberately delivered in dedication to light.

And so, still within the flames, I made this choice. Again and again. As the cycles of pain continued unrelenting, slowly my spirit began to rise beyond the pain, the fear, the sense of victimhood; beyond anything that could separate the knowing of my self as love and light. I saw how often in my past I had felt powerless, felt that things had been done to me, felt fear and helplessness in the face of what seemed to be outside forces or influences, people, situations, experiences even within my own body: anything I had perceived as being imposed upon me, or beyond my control.

As I kept choosing light, kept choosing love, gradually all the history of abdication began to dissolve. To die, truly. Never had anything been done to me, I was in full agreement with all the scenes and participants upon the stage of my entire life, lovingly enacted for my own higher purposes and evolution. I was so much more than just this body! I felt my beingness as vast, powerful—even as my physical self continued to be eaten away by pain and physical suffering. There was nothing anyone or anything could do to the true me that wasn't completely within the fullness of my immense totality. I had a hand in every beautifully choreographed moment of my life in order to realize, to the marrow of my experience, that what I am is light, is love.

Staring fear in the face, staring death in the face, staring unspeakable pain in the face—and choosing to include it all in light, in love. Choosing not just once and having it be over, but choosing, with each cycle of pain, again and again and again and again and again … each new NOW moment requiring the conscious choice, requiring the conscious reaching, walking through the doorway into light, into love. No longer needing a happy ending, because there is no ending, just the ongoing choice, ever available, ever fresh, ever there, of light. Of love.

And so—the dying of fear, of victimhood, regret, resentment, eventually ran its course into the conscious birthing of a larger space felt as infinite light and a merging oneness of love. The expansion of what became a greater consciousness—of my Self—began to fully birth. The world no longer held any threats—everything in the world was within this light, was included in love.

What could ever harm me? Kill the body, no problem! Because I am not this body, this personality, this (her)story of me. I am light. I am love. All I know, all I experience, all I see, I choose to know within light, within love.

Finally, finally, in the early hours of dawn, I went back to bed. I lay there as the pain continued its cycles, although needing slightly less writhing, slightly less panting, before it would subside.

But then the tension in my chest, that scary pain that kept sending me to the emergency room, started a faint gathering. As my awareness registered the new sensations, I could feel the fear tickling up in me.

I know myself as light. I know myself as love. Focused on my chest now, I again chose to know light. To choose light over fear, love over panic. If this is my crossover, fine. If this is my body's transition, OK. It's only a body and I am far more than just this body.

Unlike previous episodes, the chest tension must not have continued because suddenly it was nine-thirty in the morning and I was waking up. Clearly, I had finally fallen asleep, and been able to get some rest. Dennis was up, tiptoeing around. "I wanted to let you sleep. Did you have a lot of pain last night?" he innocently asked.

I closed my eyes. "Yes. I went through quite the process."

Although physically wrung out, it was OK to get up. I ran a hot bath, removed my nightclothes, gingerly stepped in. My body, which over the past months had become so thin, looked pale and delicate under the water. Ethereal. New. The nerves in my face were calm; my chest was still slightly anxious, but holding stability. I know myself as light, I know myself as love. Right now. And now. And now. And now.

It seemed I had transited the dark night and emerged. The death had taken place, the transfiguration passed through. No longer just a parable, I had walked through the fire with total conscious immersion—and out of the ashes, was now reborn. This new becoming completely unknown, a mystery—to be revealed as each new NOW moment brought the choice, once again. Walk through the door into light. Into love. Know myself as Light, as Love. This is who I AM.

The Self who dwells in the body
Is inviolable, forever.
Birthless, primordial,
It does not die when the body dies.
In the night of all beings, the wise man
Sees only the radiance of the Self.
(Bhagavad Gita, Stephen Mitchell translation)

15

A JOURNEY BACK TO WHOLENESS

Megan Fluke

When I was thirteen years old, five girls whom I considered my closest friends at the small Catholic grade school we attended cornered me in the bathroom during recess. The most outspoken of the group, Leah, grabbed my hair at the root of my scalp and started banging my head against a metal paper towel dispenser as she shouted in my ear, "If you would just start standing up for yourself and push back, I will stop!"

I've heard this all my life: that I need to toughen up and defend myself. But I was taught that if someone behaved poorly, it was because of their own pain, and I should never stoop to their level. I had not yet learned how to set personal boundaries. I accepted her attack and ran away the moment she let go.

This incident was on par with most of my lived experience starting in preschool extending through my young adulthood. All I really remember from preschool is that two girls in my class continually rejected my asking if I could play with them and I felt very alone on the playground. I had persistent head lice in fourth grade and the parents of my classmates told them not to get anywhere near me. The name "lice girl" stuck for years. I told a friend in sixth grade that I wanted to be an actress and she replied, "You are too ugly."

A group of boys in seventh grade regularly jeered that I smelled bad and lived in the sewers. (They usually added that I had a pet alligator that I rode to school and had named Frederick, the creative detail of this imagery was at least impressive.)

I walked into eighth grade after going to the restroom and a boy threw dozens of sheets of my classwork onto the ground; classmates just watched as I picked them up. For years, my closest friend in after-school care told me that we were to be "secret friends" and that I was not to talk with her when other classmates were around. While matters did seem to improve when I shifted to a larger public high school, one of my best friends told me that she would be perfect if she just had my body and her face. Boys regularly reminded me of how ugly I was.

I don't remember ever telling my parents; I think because I internalized such a profound self-loathing at a young age, I felt like I deserved to be treated poorly.

I believe the root of the bullying was because of how my then undiagnosed ADHD and celiac disease impacted my mental health and physical appearance. My ability to focus was a constant battle, excruciating stomach cramps and vomiting were a normal part of my experience, my face was puffy and acne-ridden, and I perpetually felt as if I was simultaneously "too much" and "not enough." No matter how hard I tried, I almost never felt like I belonged. Still, looking back, I fondly recall the guardian angels along my journey including mentors, parents, teachers, and friends who proactively took steps to make me feel fully loved. I wish my younger self had the tools to pay far more attention to them and far less attention to my detractors. Thankfully many of them are still in my life and today they know how much of a difference their care made.

These early wounds shaped me and I entered adulthood believing that I was fundamentally flawed. I was hyper-fixated on being liked by everyone I interacted with and desperately sought external validation. A prototypical pleaser, one of the only times a boss gave me a stern talking-to was when a coworker complained of me being "too nice" at the coffee shop we worked at when I was nineteen. While I had friends, what I brought to every relationship was the assumption that I was not worthy of them and I would rightfully get hurt. In college and after graduation, I actively sought out and pushed myself to excel in leadership roles in part to assure that as few people as possible would be in a position to hurt me. This coping mechanism worked to my advantage and I progressed quickly in local nonprofit director-level roles for most of my twenties and thirties.

Seeking a conventional sense of security, I leaped from one romantic partner to another, convinced that marriage would make me whole. I was engaged when I was twenty-three and married at twenty-four to a wonderful man who was just as stubborn and opinionated as I was. We drove one another mad. Our frequent arguments left me in tears, and my feelings of inadequacy persisted.

Our union blessed us with a perfect daughter. It was in this experience of unconditional love for Amelia that the chapter of my own healing started. The tensions in our marriage quickly became difficult to ignore and I realized that I was not living the life I wished to model for her. But I didn't know what needed to change.

On the morning of my thirtieth birthday, I took myself for a walk at dawn along a grassy hillside surrounded by oak trees.

The trees seemed to sing in a chorus that morning: "Our job is to just be. We are perfect exactly as we are. You are no different." My face heated up and tears welled in my eyes. It became glaringly clear how I had squandered decades fixated on feelings of ugliness, inadequacy, and unworthiness. I was trapped in an endless cycle of negative self-talk and the need for external affirmation. I did not want to turn forty and look back on another decade of self-loathing. I wanted to be an example for my daughter and for her to live a life delighted by her inherent worth.

This realization was the beginning of a journey that would take most of a decade to manifest. I started by focusing on my physical health because it was easier, and it provided immediate existential and physical relief. I had been perpetually pudgy and bloated since the age of two and had convinced myself that fitness was personally unattainable. I couldn't run more than a couple of blocks without getting painfully out of breath and most meals made me feel sick. I did the research, joined a gym, became a runner, and changed my diet. After cutting gluten out, my body no longer seemed regularly inflamed and I wasn't sick as often because I was finally treating my celiac disease, albeit unintentionally. It took nearly a year, but I became an athlete. For the first time in my life, I recognized the person looking back at me in the mirror.

I started to pay closer attention to other aspects of my life that needed to change. That summer, I went to therapy for the first time. After expressing how unhappy I was in my marriage, my therapist posed a profound question: "What does your body want?" Her query struck me to my core, revealing a shocking truth—I didn't think my needs and desires mattered. Without hesitation, I responded, "My body doesn't want to remain in this marriage." A few weeks later I asked for a divorce.

After processing the divorce, I started to focus on cultivating a more meaningful relationship with myself and healthier relationships with others. I initiated a book club, took philosophy classes, got a singing instructor, started skateboarding again, enjoyed concerts, and went out dancing.

My path eventually led me to a man who saw the best in me. He brought two perfect children from a previous marriage into my life. Blending our families allowed me to unconditionally love his children in addition to my own daughter with the intensity and authenticity I had always yearned for. Our relationship and our blended family thrive on trust, gentleness, and fun. The number one rule in our home is to "be yourself."

Now at thirty-seven, I feel like I am tying up loose ends of this life-altering and life-affirming decade.

At the beginning of this year, I embarked on the most restrictive elimination diet I have ever undertaken, guided by a doctor to uncover the foods that fuel me and the foods that hurt me. I want to finally heal my gut after years of my now-diagnosed celiac disease, which had damaged my small intestine and hindered nutrient absorption. My stomach aches have subsided, and regular vomiting is a thing of the past. For the first time in my life, I've only felt sick to my stomach a few days of the year rather than most.

Shortly after I uncovered the right foods for my body, I was diagnosed with and started treatment for ADHD. I am so appreciative of how many resources there are out there for people who are not neurotypical and the support of my family and friends as I stop trying to force myself to "be normal."

With the realization that I needed more spaciousness to focus on my mental health, I decided to leave the fulfilling role as the executive director of Green Foothills, an incredible local environmental nonprofit. After ten years of service that fueled my sense of identity and purpose, this move was a testament to my allowing myself to rest and fully embody the wisdom of the trees that spoke to me on my birthday: I am perfect simply as I am. This professional transition was also terrifying because I had no idea what I was going to do next.

A well-worded LinkedIn search gifted me with the connection of a career coach who billed herself as a "Creativity Coach and Life Strategist." Perhaps even more important than helping me figure out what was next for me professionally, she included a complimentary mental fitness program as part of her offering. Through this well-timed six-week program, I unexpectedly came face-to-face with the hurt little girl in me. She appears in the form of my preschool-aged self, wearing long hair that had never been cut, in the dress I wore on the day that I was first made fun of by two girls in my class.

I realized that this little version of myself was almost always my ill-suited protector in stressful moments. She would encourage me to use her weapons of tears, tantrums, or running away. As part of an exercise in the program, I let her know that she was worthy of and had my unconditional love, that she was finally safe, that no one was going to hurt her anymore. Most importantly for me today, I let her know that she didn't need to protect me or anyone any longer. Her job is to play and to remind me to have fun and enjoy my life. I visit little Megan regularly in the corner of my mind where she will forever be able to laugh and swing on a playground, enjoying the drumbeat of love and support among her peers, as the sun perpetually sets on what was for her an absolutely perfect day. I am so thankful that she is at peace now and that I'm now uncovering my grown-up inner voice.

My journey has not been linear, and I still struggle with anxiety and feelings of self-doubt. But I am finally at peace with who I am. I am cultivating a deeper spiritual practice and am finding avenues to express myself and let my light shine. Soon I will have a finished large tattoo on my shoulder depicting a wild, angelic woman accompanied by a lioness with the backdrop of a large oak tree. Together they symbolize everything I aspire to always be: a powerful, unapologetic woman who knows her inherent self-worth.

As I look ahead toward my continued evolution, I am confronting my deep-seated trust issues that formed after the traumatic experiences of my childhood. I am just finally starting to accept that the world is not out to get me, and I can indeed trust almost everyone, especially other women. I treasure the friends I have, and I feel treasured by them. Recently I joyously accepted an invitation to join a group of women who get together to skateboard. It feels revolutionary to be in a femme community gathering together to have fun, learn, and cheer one another on in our respective awesomeness.

In the words of Sri Sri Ravi Shankar, "Find the love you seek, by first finding the love within yourself. Learn to rest in that place within you that is your true home." This is what I finally know at my core: The most significant relationship we will ever have, is the one with ourselves. Genuine love in relationship with others flows from a place of wholeness, not lack. We are each individually complete. Today I finally see and accept myself for the divine being I am.

16

MY MIDLIFE INITIATION

Vanessa Nixon

Between the years 2018 and 2020 I turned fifty, completed my journey through menopause, navigated a divorce after eighteen years of marriage, bought a house, and started dating for the first time in twenty-five years. When I tell people this story they comment on my bravery. It didn't feel brave at the time. It felt like my life was spiraling out of control and I was hanging on for dear life!

While it was very overwhelming and painful at times, I see now my experiences provided me with the opportunity to create something new in almost every area of my life. I found that I could create this next chapter of my life and step into my power more fully. I could bring my gifts out into the world in alignment with my desires, passions, gifts, and wisdom. I could walk in the flow of wellness, health, and vitality.

I never expected that the most intense challenges of my life would lead me to feel so empowered, so energized and so confident in who I am … who I truly am. Looking back, I realize that I became my most authentic self in the midst of that two-year crucible. I came out of that time feeling so confident in my ability to tap into my inner wisdom …to heal myself, my family, and my clients in a truly magical way.

This journey of transformation through natural healing began almost thirty years ago. In my youth, I struggled with chronic, recurring bouts of bronchitis for years. From the age of fifteen to twenty-one, I had been on a downward spiral of illness. I caught every cold that came around and each time, it went deep into my chest and developed into bronchitis.

I still vividly recall waking up every morning after a scant few hours of sleep, coughing until my sides ached, my ribs felt bruised, and I was too weak to move. As a teenager, one of my worst fears was having a coughing attack in the middle of class and having to rush out of the room, eyes streaming, barely able to catch my breath between coughs and ending up in the bathroom, my chest spasming with pain and my coughing turning to retching. I had been given all the conventional treatments, including multiple rounds of antibiotics on a regular basis and codeine cough syrup, but my health continued to decline.

In my early twenties, my friend David noticed that I was taking antibiotics every day and asked why. When I told him my story, he asked me a question nobody had ever asked me before. "Is it working?"

I had never thought to ask myself that question and when I pondered it, I realized that, no, it was not working. And that sparked a series of other questions in my mind …

- If this is not working, is there another option?
- Is there more than one option?
- If so, what are they?

As the daughter of a nurse, I had been deeply entrenched in the conventional medical model growing up and I had no idea there were other methods of health care. That one question—"Is it working?"—opened my mind to the idea of other possibilities and for the first time in many years, I dared hope that things could be different.

David shared that when he got sick, he often went to see an herbalist and asked if I would like to be introduced to her. I had never even heard of herbal medicine before and was intrigued. Within a few weeks, I was sick yet again and decided to take him up on his offer. I went to see his herbalist and she gave me a remedy formulated for respiratory illness. To my delight and amazement, what had previously taken me eight weeks of recovery time took only two weeks with the herbal formula. And, even more amazingly, the recurrences became less and less frequent until bronchitis became a thing of the past.

That did it! I was hooked. I began my journey of creating a natural lifestyle and maintaining true wellness for myself no matter what health challenges I faced. And I am pleased to report that I have not had a bout of bronchitis in almost twenty years.

After healing myself from chronic respiratory illnesses, I began devouring every book I could get my hands on that might help me understand why the herbal remedy I took was so effective. I started a course of self-study in herbalism with the works of Susun Weed and Rosemary Gladstar, among many others, and soon enrolled in official herbal studies courses with well-renowned herbalist Cascade Anderson Geller. That led me to understand that what I had been eating all my life needed close inspection … which led me to other natural modalities … and still other natural healing methods. Soon, I was experiencing such a different lifestyle that I hardly remembered what it had been like to suffer as I had for so many years. My energy levels, productivity, creativity, and joy were at such a high level on a daily basis that my old life seemed like it had been lived by someone else. Sure, I still came down with a cold every once in a while, but the difference was that now, I had the confidence and skills to heal myself quickly and the wisdom to listen to what my body needed in the moment.

So, when I entered the waters of perimenopause, I expected smooth sailing. Ha! If only I knew then what I know now. Even though I came into menopause with three decades of practicing optimal nutrition, herbal medicine, flower essences, and homeopathy to raise my general level of health to an incredibly high standard, I still experienced unexpected challenges when I hit menopause.

The mood swings and emotional outbursts I experienced really caught me by surprise. Even though I had always had "the gift of tears" (as a good friend and client once called it), I found myself crying at the most inopportune moments. Even though I had always considered myself to be extremely patient, I found my patience wearing thin. And even though I was confident in my ability to manage my personal relationships with relative ease, I found myself in a marriage that was hurtful, unsupportive, and at a dead end. I found myself living with a constant knot in my belly, not knowing where I was going to end up or how to make sure my children were not traumatized in the process of an agonizing divorce.

So, my marriage of more than eighteen years ended in divorce. I moved to a new town and bought my own home all on my own. Meanwhile, my eldest two daughters moved out of the family home and I began to focus on my career for the first time in twenty years. My children were launched, I started dating, and I fully embraced my menopausal self. Talk about a whirlwind!

But there was one thing that made the difference for me and helped me start to turn everything around. When things were the most difficult and I was struggling the most … I remembered that I had resources. I had tools and techniques, and most of all I had support.

I had women friends I could lean on. I had mentors who provided safe spaces for me to process what I was going through so I could move forward. I had my education in nutrition, herbal medicine, flower essences, homeopathy, aromatherapy, and reflexology to lean on. And I had a connection to my inner healer, my intuition, my innate wisdom to know what my mind, body, and soul needed to move me forward and elevate my life to a new level, a new place of health, fulfillment, and abundance I had never experienced before.

So, I can honestly say that I've been through the initiation. I've been through fire and I came out on the other side. And I can see that every piece of what I have experienced was an opportunity. An opportunity for growth, an opportunity for healing, and an opportunity to share my gifts with others and truly make a positive difference in their lives. Maybe the best part of this entire journey is that I was forged by fire in my midlife journey, and I discovered a passion for helping other women do the same.

Another thing that I discovered along the way was that many women have similar experiences as they journey through the transition from perimenopause, through menopause and into postmenopause. But most of them have not had the privilege of coming into this phase of life with a high level of health to begin with, or with a support system to draw from, so they are often really suffering. The symptoms they experience sometimes keep them in bed all day, lead them to withdraw from their social life, and weaken their connection to their bodies and minds. Too many women have even confided that they feel like they are losing their minds. They fear for their health, and their future, and they don't know where to turn.

Without a doubt, each woman's path through midlife is her own and unique. But if there's anything I know for certain, it's that we all need resources to flourish at this potent time of life. We all need the support of other wise women, and when we have these supports in place, there is nothing we cannot do, be, have, or create in our lives.

17

ORANGE

Susan Bloch

In the pedestrian street of my local London market, I close my eyes and rub my thumbs over the crepe-textured tangerine skin cocooned in the palms of my hands. My fingers slide over the peel, caressing each ridge and wrinkle. I lift the fruit to my nose and breathe in, long and deep, hoping the sharp citrus scent might bring John back to me. Or at least some part of him—his breath on my neck and his warm palms over mine.

"Such a lovely man, we do miss him," calls Bob, the vendor from our favorite stall. "I loved our chats."

He stands under a canvas awning behind his table, filling baskets with apples, pears, and oranges. He wipes his hands on a blue-and-white checked apron and looks up at me. "Gonna rain any minute … fed up with this grey … got a brolly with you? You doing OK, love?"

I start to tell Bob that I'm settling down all right, but I can't find the words to pretend. The lump in my throat feels as if I've tried to swallow a whole kumquat, and I can scarcely breathe, never mind talk. My fists clench the tangerine until I become aware of the juice trickling down my forearms and inside my shirtsleeves. Bob leans over the table and touches my wrists.

"It gets better," he says trying to look into my tear-filled eyes, but I can't meet his gaze. Bob continues to pile apples, oranges, potatoes, and broccoli in baskets, tempting me to fill my own shopping bag, but then I remember– there's only one of us now. I can't be bothered to shop for myself.

On Saturday mornings, John and I enjoyed shopping for our fruit and vegetables at this Islington market together. We picked shiny Granny Smith apples, breathed in the aroma of fresh parsley and celery, and scooped handfuls of beans and brussels sprouts into brown paper bags for Bob to weigh. But it was my John who always chose the citrus, rubbing the tips of his fingers over the dimpled skin. He'd describe the color each week as if it were sacred. And to him, it was almost holy.

"The color this week is deeper," or "it's almost reddish," or "almost lemony," he'd say.

As a child, it was an orange that brought color into his life for the very first time. John grew up in Bolton, a cotton-milling town near Manchester, England. He described never-ending gray skies with smoke billowing from chimney stacks and soot smothering oak trees and privet hedges. Stray cotton threads—a soporific haze, dank and dim—infiltrated people's lungs, causing hacking coughs.

"There was food rationing after the Second World War and everything was pale. We ate white bread with margarine the color of sickly school paste; beige Spam and sallow powdered scrambled eggs; boiled potatoes, cabbage, and turnips. When I was seven, I saw my first orange," John said. "And it was as if I saw color for the first time."

My childhood was nothing like his. In South Africa, I grew up with plenty of sunlight, purple jacaranda trees, and crimson and magenta bougainvillea. All kinds of produce filled the fruit and vegetable store: papayas, apricots, mangoes, and mulberries; tomatoes, pumpkins, broccoli, and zucchini. It was difficult to think of life with ashen skies and bland food. My heart filled with compassion for the boy John, deprived of such simple delights.

"One of our neighbors bought one orange," John said. "It was a spectacle; we'd heard about them, but never seen or eaten one. They put the fruit on their kitchen table, and every day we crowded in to marvel at it. We could only stare at it as no one was allowed to touch it. After a week or so, the skin turned gray and moldy. No one suggested peeling it to look inside and worse, no one even tasted it."

Decades later, every time we came home from our Saturday market shopping, the first thing John did was slice into an orange. Eating citrus was a divine experience, tangible proof that he was no longer that boy stuck in a polluted, war-exhausted town. Now months after John's death, I stand on the bustling market street holding that tangerine, as if John is here with me, cradled against my lips. I almost hear him and Bob discussing the Brexit shenanigans as he pays for our purchases.

Suddenly dizzy, I grab on to a canopy pole to stop myself from falling over. Bob helps other customers, taking their cash and doling out change. Perhaps he's still yelling, "Oranges, three for a pound," but I don't hear him. Nor do I wipe the rain off my cheeks. Someone pushes me into the stall table, but I don't offer a dirty look or say, "No pushing, please."

I place the squishy tangerine back onto the table and turn away to get back onto the street. Smells of pungent mushrooms, acrid onions, and garlic from a nearby stall follow me as I turn away. Back on the main street, drizzle drips down the back of my neck. My shopping bag is empty as I walk home.

18

WHAT THE MOUNTAIN REVEALS

Jnana Gowan

"It is what the mountain reveals to us that has any lasting value." This quote is written on a Post-it above my desk, embellished in my email signature, and attached to the footer of my newsletter. I cannot recall where I first came across it, but this quote became my guiding principle.

One of my earliest childhood memories was getting my first glimpse of the Rocky Mountains at the tender age of three and a half. My sister, my parents, and I had piled into our blue Ford station wagon and driven for what seemed like a lifetime from Southern Indiana, crossing the especially long and flat state of Kansas, heading toward the explosive geography of Colorado.

Awaiting the mountains' magnificent presence on the horizon was a test of patience for everyone in that car. But the first sight of those towering mountains filled me with awe. They spoke to me then and they speak to me now. Throughout my life, I have been cultivating and nourishing my relationship with them and seeking their wisdom.

Why look to the mountains for a message of lasting value? Many years after writing that quote on a Post-it, I fell in love with and gained spiritual sustenance from a Peruvian tradition where I learned how to honor mountains as ancient ones that influence our daily lives.

From an Andean lens, mountains are known as apus (ah-pooz). The word apu encompasses not just the physical form of the mountain, but also includes its nature being and consciousness, which are seen as highly important participants of all life. Some believe that apus, or mountain lords, were once humans of a saintlike status. Upon completion of their earth-walk as a human, they reincarnate as the consciousness of a particular mountain. In this way, they continue to be of service to humanity and the natural world.

Apus are the world's first point of contact with the heavenly beings of the upper world, or the hanaq pacha, and receive blessings and energy from the above. One could say the mountains are like the pump house; as the energies from the heavens filter down to the planet, the apus distribute this highly refined, spiritual energy across the planet for our growth and healing. It is our job to acknowledge and honor these beneficent ones in exchange for this offering. We do this by way of pilgrimage, physical offerings, and prayerful connection.

My "lasting value" story has two parts, which occurred a little more than a year apart from one another and has to do with two mountains.

Part 1, pre-COVID, September 2019, MACHU PICCHU, PERU. Earlier that year I asked Juan, a medicine man from Aguas Calientes, if he would help my husband, Jeff, and I commemorate twenty years of marriage. The magic and power of Peru and its traditions have shaped and healed my life and dictated who I have become. I wanted to share the beauty of these powerful lands with my husband at this pivotal time in our lives.

Juan welcomed us and made arrangements. The night before our visit to Machu Picchu, Juan created a despacho to sanctify the beginning of our time together. A despacho is a sacred offering or gratitude bundle. As preparation for our journey, he requested that we pass the bundle between us in the night, sleeping with it under our heads, and bringing it to him in the morning. At predawn, we greeted him in the lobby, and we made our way to the bus that would make its climbing way to the base of Machu Picchu.

Early in our ascent, we imbibed the sacrament of huachuma, San Pedro cactus, then climbed the uneven steps and for nearly five miles continued up and up to almost eight thousand feet above sea level. We were, to say the least, in an altered state. As we neared the top, Juan cleared away a few branches revealing a very small private ledge off the path.

"We'll do our ceremony here," he said.

On the ledge, he rattled and whistled, speaking to the mountain and nature helpers, inviting them to join and bless us. We did not realize until the ceremony was well underway, that we were getting married again, renewing our vows, and our life path together. Juan brought breath and power to this special moment and, as witness, a hummingbird perched on a branch above our heads.

At one point, as we stood back-to-back on the ledge, Juan placed a wand of condor tail feathers between us. Jeff and I worked to maintain balance as he began working the condor feathers on my shoulder blades poking and slightly pinching. It wasn't unpleasant, but it felt odd. He had us turn to face one another, our hands holding the despacho, acknowledging this time as a marker in our history, a commemoration and celebration of all that has passed, so that now, we would go forward anew.

Juan completed the ceremony by offering the despacho into the folds of the mountain at our marital site. Back on the path, the mist that had enshrouded us all morning had lifted, and we could see how far we had come in so many ways. It was a magnificent wedding gift from Spirit, and we made our way to the summit for the newlywed photo opp. It was pretty freaking awesome, I'll tell you.

Later that evening at the retreat center as we readied for bed, I asked Jeff what he thought of Juan with the condor feathers working the shoulder blades. Jeff said that he hadn't noticed anything. At that moment my innards lit up as I realized that part of the ceremony was for me. I had a deep knowing, met with excitement, that on Machu Picchu my condor wings had been activated and it was time for me to fly!

This activation was confirmation that a change in my life's work was coming and the wings were here to launch it. We left Aguas Calientes in a renewed state. We received the gifts of the mountain, shepherded by Juan, to grow wings and begin a new chapter together—both individually and as a couple.

Part 2: November 2020, Mount Tamalpais, (Mount Tam) MARIN COUNTY, CALIFORNIA. Mount Tam, along with Mount Diablo, are the regional apus of the San Francisco Bay Area, acknowledged as sacred places of healing and sustenance for peoples of the past and present.

In September I had honorably parted ways with my teacher, don Oscar. I had been in his sphere of teachings for many years, the last five of which I taught a fifteen-month intensive Peruvian shamanic apprenticeship program. For more than a decade, his organization was inextricably woven into my identity, my community, and my spiritual practice, but it was time for me to move on.

Eight weeks post-Peru marked a new chapter for me and I felt Mount Tam calling me. I had just completed a hypnotherapy certification program. For two years I searched for a program where I could integrate my shamanic skills and spiritual background into the course, a place where I wouldn't feel like a weirdo. I was thrilled to find my people, find my place and complete the program.

I felt a sense of accomplishment and gratitude, yet mostly I felt change. It was as if I was back on that ledge on Machu Picchu, only this time, I was stepping off the side of the mountain, testing my new condor wings.

It truly was a leap of faith because something new was happening, but it was not here yet: As I drove up the mountain, it got progressively foggier, and then it began to drizzle. Marin County was like a dry sponge, having not seen precipitation in the Bay Area for ten months. The sky opened up as I pulled into the parking lot, and it began raining hard. This was the promise of change and excitement: new, clean, fresh.

I parked, pulled on my rain jacket, and made my way to a large stone outcropping. Like on Machu Picchu, I brought a completed despacho and offered my heartfelt thanks for this swirl of change I was in. I said my prayers of thanks and slipped the despacho under a small bolder. "Thank you, for every blessing in my life. Thank you for guiding me, thank you for helping me not feel so alone," I said.

As I stood in the rain my senses were enlivened by the intoxicating essence of petrichor. It was as if the mountain and all the inhabitants were rejoicing in the rainfall; the birds, the beetles, and the branches were all saying, "Yes please, it's been so long, we are so happy to see you."

I began walking the trail and noticed that because of the dense canopy the ground was still dry. I pulled the jacket hood off my head, craving to be drenched by falling water. Ten months without rain will do that to you. I longed for a limpia, a cleansing, to be wiped off, clean and clear, and ready for the next thing. In this moment of reverie, I saw water accumulating on the dry path, these droplets finding one another, forming a snakelike line, and beginning to flow. This got my full attention.

For years, one of my consistent prayers was to be in the flow. Right here, the mountain was showing me, "Open your eyes, this is flow." I stopped and studied this ancient conversation between the sky and earth; the above and the below. No longer interested in hiking, I wanted to eavesdrop on this conversation and see how it may apply to my life.

All my senses were awake: the smells, sights, and sounds. I felt a deep sense of connection to the earth and all her elements and my good fortune to witness and participate in this beautiful dance. What auspicious timing! My condor wings were unfolding on this day of change, and I felt certain that I could fly in the rain.

I had the mountain to myself and as the rain increased, the flow intensified, steady and always finding its way. When an obstacle presents itself in the path of flow, the water simply aligns to the way of least resistance. How can I do that? Sometimes the obstacle isn't physical but one of the heart. For example, something inside said it was time to move on, to let go, and to change. That meant I had to leave the tradition, the teaching, the community, and the container I'd been in for well over a decade. I was being asked to trust in the very alive, very awake Universe and go with the flow even though I had no idea what was next. I was called to spread new wings and to stay with the path that had the most energy. I reminded myself that to trust, not resist, and keep going was a good plan.

I followed the stream as it grew, still just a trickle, but the medicine was strong, and I took it in, slowed down. This is what nature offers us: presence. Here-ness. Wakefulness, as in: "Wake up to this moment!" This moment offered no planning, no picture taking, and no to-do lists. Just here.

My heart was jumping. My smile was an extension of my unbounded excitement at being aware and alive in this slice of time. Such an honor. The Quechua word ayni, came to me. Ayni meaning "sacred reciprocity." Ayni is a life principle for Andean people and roughly translates as "today for you, tomorrow for me." This principle governs life in all ways: all relationships of human, animal, earth, and star connection.

The despacho I offered at the beginning of my journey on Apu Tamalpais was filled with prayers of gratitude for everything in my life and the abundant support I received from the natural world. This ritualized act/expression of ayni creates balance.

When making offerings we acknowledge our place with nature-beings and say, "Yes, we are connected." As we awaken to the natural world, the natural world awakens to us. Yet we have forgotten this conversation, that we are woven into the great web of life together. Various original peoples have stated that Western culture is in a great slumber; a dormancy regarding earth-honoring traditions, rituals, and practices. We have work to do, reparations of our mistreatment and abuse, and separation from our Mother Earth. Yet, like a beautiful and loving mother, she continually leans back into us, happy to see us saying, "Today for you, tomorrow for me."

In exchange for my gifts, observation, and presence, the mountain responded, "Pay attention and receive a road map to life. Settle down, stop, listen, smell, see, breathe, flow. Sometimes the flow seems to stagnate (settle down, stop), yet with time it builds up (stop, listen, breathe), and the path resumes."

Machu Picchu gave me my condor wings and Mount Tamalpais has shown me how to use them. Honoring these sacred mountains bestowed a transformational wisdom, giving me the lasting value of putting me directly on my life's path of purpose.

19

DESTINY

Thea Iberall

I was living in Southern California finishing an MFA and decided to write a one-woman show. About relationships. Now, I consider myself a stable person. My first relationship lasted eighteen years, my second for eleven years. And then my life went off the rails as I got involved with controlling women, jealous women, passive-aggressive women, players. My heart was torn to shreds and I swore I'd never be in another relationship. Ever. I'd sail into my old age alone. And to remind myself of this, I wrote my one-woman show.

Then I had to go to Massachusetts for a conference, and I asked my friends Mary and Dianna to gather people so I could try out my one-woman show material on a friendly audience.

So, there I was in their living room talking about how my heart was broken. "Lovesickness. It's like a heart attack, the doctors say, the same tightness in the chest, the gasping for breath. Your chest feels like a broken drum, with moaned myocytes, and hydrophilic heat. They say limerence is the technical term for being in love. How it demands her uninflected breath curling around you."

Suddenly, there was a thud. Someone in the audience had fallen off the couch. Everyone laughed. The woman who fell was embarrassed. All I thought was, groupies—they're worse than controlling, jealous, passive-aggressive players.

Shirley said it was my words that were like a bolt of energy that lifted her up off the couch. She invited me to lunch the next day at a Thai restaurant. And sitting in a wooden booth in the back, I could feel the energy between us. It was like the air was vibrating. I took her two hands in mine across the table, and it was like a circuit completed.

In Judaism, there is a term beshert, which means "inevitable" or "destiny." It's the hidden power believed to control what will happen in the future. Like providence or kismet.

Shirley is my beshert. We were destined to meet, but it had to be the right time, when we were both ready.

Because there is more to this story. Remember my friends Mary and Dianna? They were one of the first lesbian couples to get married in the state in 2004. I've known Mary for thirty years, and she invited me to their wedding. Dianna has known Shirley forty years, since the Brownies and she invited Shirley. Shirley and I both sat at the friends' table. I was sitting next to my ex. Shirley sat with her life partner. We didn't talk. I remember thinking she looked angry.

I also remember what Rector Paul said when he quoted Baal Shem Tov. "From every human being there rises a light that reaches straight to heaven. And when two souls that are destined to be together find each other, their streams of light flow together and a single, brighter light goes forth from their united being."

Unfortunately, Shirley's partner was killed in a car accident, and she spent a year making peace with her grief and changing her life.

And then one night, she stood in her backyard and raised her fist to the sky. "I don't want to live my life alone," she yelled. "I've accepted what happened, I'm cooperating, and I want your support."

We met in Mary and Diana's living room a week later.

We are each other's beshert, only it took time for it to happen. We both needed to work on ourselves and learn our life lessons. I truly had to let go of trying to find love and trying to have a relationship. I had to be alone to discover the real me. I had to connect to my heart.

This destiny took the power of words, the courage to say yes to love again, and the willingness to work on ourselves. And when our streams of light were ready to flow together, the Universe made it happen (seventeen years ago).

20

UNITED AT LAST

Kim Jellicoe

As I sat in my window seat looking out over the clouds above Nebraska, I reflected on my life. I had turned forty the previous year. Forty. That's the year when you can no longer ask what you are going to do or be when you grow up. It has happened. You have grown up. As I sat on the plane, I reflected that this was definitely not where, or who, I thought I would be.

On that flight from San Francisco to Chicago in August of 2009, I let the truth settle in. I had always assumed I'd get married and have a family. But the way my life was going, it looked like I would probably not get married or even find a loving partnership.

"And I have no Plan B," I thought wistfully. I had my career, my friends, my family, and my interests, all of which I loved. But … was there nothing that could more deeply nourish my soul? I couldn't think of anything, and so my future lay before me as empty as the expanse of sky outside the plane.

I stared out the window and cycled through ideas of what could give my life meaning.

"I'll just try to be happy," I thought.

My internal editor rejected that idea immediately. Happiness, as a concept, is too ephemeral. And I don't even want to be "happy" all the time. Life is full of ups and downs, and I love that richness.

"What about if I just notice when I'm happy? If I'm enjoying the view out the window, I'll pause and appreciate it," I pondered. "If I like the taste of a glass of wine, I'll take a moment to appreciate that, too. Each time I'm happy, I'll just stop and notice."

I took a deep breath in and breathed out a sigh. Yes, that seemed like a realistic, albeit humble, life aspiration. Somewhat satisfied with my new Plan B, I went back to gazing out the window and thinking about the upcoming week in Chicago, with my dad.

On a phone call earlier that year, my seventy-three-year-old father had shared that it was one of the "great tragedies" of his life that he had never seen a baseball game at Wrigley Field. So I arranged for us to spend a week in Chicago to watch the legendary Cubs. The Cubbies lost to the Pirates in the twelfth inning, but Cubs fans did not disappoint; they cheered and sang all the way through the bottom of the twelfth.

I loved spending time with my dad, but after a week I was exhausted. I decided this would be a good time to use my frequent flier miles to upgrade to business class to enjoy a glass of wine and a nice meal. I also knew that I had a big commitment the following Saturday; I was to officiate my friends Mark and Rebecca's wedding. I had written a draft of the ceremony but hadn't committed it to memory yet. The flight home would provide me with four and a half hours of uninterrupted time to concentrate. So I put my speech in my carry-on and packed my suitcase.

United Airlines had recently started charging fees in addition to miles to upgrade. I needed that glass of wine, so I paid seventy-five dollars and ten thousand miles and secured my seat. 8G. Unfortunately, I couldn't get a window seat, but I had managed the upgrade, so I'd have to be satisfied with the aisle. I drove to the airport, dropped off my rental car, checked in, and waited at the gate to board my flight.

I was committed to not talking to anyone on the flight, not only to prepare for the wedding but also to recover from my exhausting trip.

"I'm going to put on my bitchiest face and not talk to anyone," I told myself as I boarded the plane.

The flight attendant smiled and said, "8G," reading from my boarding pass as she directed me to the second aisle. I maneuvered around the galley and headed down the aisle. Six, seven, ugh! Someone was sitting in 8G. Worse yet, he was smiling at me!

Bitchy face. Bitchy tone. You can do this …

I conjured up my coldest tone. "I think you're sitting in my seat," I said sternly.

"Oh, I'm sorry!" he exclaimed in a slight English accent. "I didn't even check. I always get the aisle." He continued on a bit confused, "Do you want the aisle?"

"No," I replied, "I actually prefer the window."

He partially stood up as I squeezed through to the window seat, retrieved the black folder with my wedding speech, and stowed my backpack under the seat in front of me.

During the preflight announcements, we each got settled in. This fellow traveler and I exchanged a few niceties, and in the process, he learned that I lived in San Mateo.

"Ah!" He seemed delighted. "I'm actually on a house-hunting trip. One of the cities I'm looking at is San Mateo."

He shared that he had printouts of available apartments in his carry-on. Despite my commitment to be antisocial, I couldn't help but be intrigued. What was this guy's story? He had an English accent. He lived in Chicago. He wanted to move to San Mateo of all places. My curiosity got the better of me, and I asked a few questions.

As we chatted about his plans and my recent week with my dad, the captain announced that they were going to have to replace a part on the plane, and our flight would be delayed. Since we were in business class, the flight attendant offered us wine, and the conversation flowed.

My seatmate shared stories about designing phones and leading teams at Motorola. I shared my plans to officiate my friends' wedding, to which he exclaimed, "I thought only priests and ship captains performed marriages!" Two and a half hours on the ground flew by, and neither of us seemed to notice when we took off. As we ascended to cruising altitude, I regaled him with my plan to swim from Alcatraz to San Francisco, and he shared stories of his distant ancestor Charlemagne.

At a certain point, the lights in the cabin dimmed. My seatmate was recounting one of his favorite stories involving Ghandi and Ghandi's grandson. He got choked up as he shared the details. I was touched by his emotional honesty.

"Oh no," I thought, "I hope he doesn't become self-conscious when he realizes he's revealed so much to me, a total stranger." But as he finished the story, he just smiled warmly, and we went on with the conversation.

"Wow," I thought, admiring his emotional realness. "He's so brave."

There in the dark with our seats reclined and sharing stories, I found myself wanting to reach over and touch his arm to make a point. But I chided myself. "Kim, don't be foolish! You don't even know his name."

As we continued to chat, I thought sadly, "Why don't I ever meet someone like this?"

The rational observer in me replied, "Well, you are meeting someone like this ..."

It was true. I didn't know what his story was, but I was grateful for the interesting conversation.

Two hours into the flight, I remembered … my speech! I had planned to use this time to memorize it. But then I also recounted my new life Plan B—to notice happiness. I noticed that I was happy talking to this stranger. So, I chose to continue noticing happiness.

We touched down after eight hours and both realized the flight and conversation were coming to an end. Amused and a bit mystified, I told him, "I don't even know your name."

He gave me his business card while telling me his name. Roger Jellicoe. I took his card and followed him down the aisle until he stopped at the exit row where a few of his colleagues were waiting. So, this was goodbye.

I felt like giving him a hug but again remembered that I barely knew him. We said goodbye awkwardly, and I proceeded up the jetway toward baggage claim.

I waited for my luggage and studied his card thinking of what a nice guy he was. I became aware of other travelers gathering. What if he came to get his suitcase and saw me staring at his card? I imagined how silly I would look. So, I tucked the card in my back pocket, collected my suitcase from the luggage belt, and hailed a taxi home.

The next day I woke up and thought about the stranger. He had told me to call him, but … it was only seven in the morning! Obviously too early to call. I'd play it cool. I'd wait until tonight, or maybe even tomorrow to call or text him.

I made it through that long day and even that night, and when I awoke the following day, I noticed I was excited at the thought of talking to the stranger again. I went to my jeans pocket to retrieve his business card, and … it wasn't there. Nooo! Where could it be? I looked through my purse, I looked in my suitcase. It was gone.

Wow. Sigh. "Well, I guess it wasn't meant to be." I shrugged and started a load of laundry. But that thought didn't sit well; it seemed like we had more to say.

I thought about trying to find his information online, but I had a problem: I couldn't remember his name! I did remember that he said he had been in Fortune magazine for his work on the Razr phone. Not having owned a Razr, I Googled "Razor Motorola Fortune Magazine." The article appeared at the top of the search results. I scrolled down and found a photo of three men with their names listed in the caption. Ah yes, Roger Jellicoe.

As a former recruiter, it shouldn't have surprised me that the receptionist at Motorola refused to share his cell phone number with me. And since he was traveling, there was no point in leaving a message at his desk. I recalled that he and I had talked about having created Facebook accounts earlier that year; in March Facebook had enabled users to post content outside their circle of friends, so the app was growing in popularity. Roger had created an account to do some testing for business, and a friend of mine had invited me to join. I hadn't used the app much, but I thought that maybe I could find him there.

I searched and found his profile. Yeah! Now what would I write? Something casual. OK. "Hi there! This is Kim from seat 8H last week. I lost your business card but found you here. Just wanted to say hi." Send.

I checked back an hour later. No reply. I checked again the next day. Still no reply. My heart sank a little. Oh well. I tried.

A few days later, I saw his reply, which started with, "I'm in England now on business and visiting friends and family." So that explained his delayed response.

That evening I went to a Giants baseball game with a group from work. I had told my colleague Carissa about Roger, so between pitches she asked, “What happened to that guy on the plane?”

A Facebook alert of a post from him had just come in, so I read it with her. It had a photo of the placard posted outside of the Eagle Pub in Cambridge where Watson and Crick had announced the structure of DNA. He had written, “I know you work at Genentech, so I thought of you when I passed this today.”

Carissa looked at me with sentiment etched all over her face. “Awe, he sounds really nice.”

Roger and I met for dinner on his next trip to San Francisco, and he moved to the Bay Area that fall. We bought a house together the following June and married two years later. We’ve now been married for eleven years, and we’ve never run out of things to say. I’m grateful every day that I’m still seated next to him. And I’m SO glad that I changed my mindset on that flight to notice happiness.

21

MAMA RUTHIE'S HOLY EXIT

Susan Shloss

12.4.2021

Mama Ruthie Is Leaving

I'm not prepared to sit around and watch you slip silently from your body
A mother is forever
From day one she's there
To depend on
Wrestle with
Love, disdain

I didn't fear her
But this moment of dissolution stirs that in me
I'm not ready

I don't know what I'd prefer
Not her suffering
Not her bare existence in late-stage Alzheimer's
Just a few more moments of her wry humor

Her candid observations, like her new best friend
whose name never did settle in her brain

"She carries her doll everywhere. It's okay."
"If you saw this place."
She tried to make it work
"I'm trying."
I want to see her pleasure, her enjoyment
Recognition of the immense love that surrounds her
What has been will have to be enough
But my heart says no, don't go, not yet

✦ ✦ ✦

12.24.2021

The Wisdom of Wailing

Since she left,
I've cried often
But last night
after a very hard day of feeling lost
a sound emerged
I let it come
A wail
Not a loud one
But definitely an organic deep
cry of anguish that freed me
more than the countless releases of feeling that bubbled up in my throat over these two weeks escaping as a shallow whimper

Years ago, I participated in an African grief ritual
There, my wailing felt forced
Self-conscious
I had not yet lost my mother
Now I know the wisdom of wailing

✦✦✦

Dear Mom

Every day (several times a day)
I think to call you
No—my body, my being is moved
Much like my impulse to go to the kitchen on my work breaks for nourishment

Sometimes it was hard to face your spiraling despair

They took my house
and my car

You were so independent
Smart
Capable

Before they took your car, your house
You lost the one thing you were still doing to engage your mind
Jurisdiction over your money

I'm sorry

When I asked about a book I'd sent, you said in a deep flat voice as if you were finally forced to say

I can't read

We used to love to talk novels

The newspaper finally stopped making sense
(Those titles are cryptic)

Still when we stopped the subscription
You asked
What happened to my newspapers?

They took my car
There was no reason!
I was stupid
I let them take my house
Mom, you had no choice
I didn't want to leave
I loved my house!

I know, it was everything

My parents took my house
How could they?
I'm so angry at them

I know, it's really hard
It was a beautiful house
It was your art project

I miss you so much
I'm calling you now

We can just chat and share the day
I feel your presence expressed through your muddled mind
Your kind and loving heart
Your care
Here's how I know how much you deeply loved each of us
How hard it was to leave us
Moments before you departed, I saw the wetness in your eyes
A tear trickling down your cheek

✦ ✦ ✦

What I Really Want to Talk About

What I really want to talk about is this life
And that I couldn't open up to you
Not really
I was too damaged, too hurt
I could never ask for your advice
I know you wanted me to

These things I fully received through you
Your love of art and beauty
Your love of nature

Maybe we can be friends now that you are free
of all that karma
The pain of what he did, what she said, what so-and-so didn't say

A legacy of insecurity, lies, and hiding out

It's all over now

What advice do you have for me?

✦ ✦ ✦

Death Speaks

On the other side of busy, death speaks

Live now, while your body breathes
Love shamelessly

Remember me
Her soul cries out

I was good!

✦ ✦ ✦

The Day She Died

12.12.2021, the day she died
Was an eleven day
Service to the divine
She didn't believe in God so much
But she lived in service

Her mind plagued her
Even before the disease took over

At times she was happier
Was it the pharma cocktail?

The end came quickly
Hospice was supposed to turn it around, give her more time
But she turned away from time

It was as if when the hospice bed arrived
she could finally let go

Near the end in a rare moment of just the two of us
She suddenly woke up, turned to me

"I've been thinking …
They took my car
They took my house
I guess I'll sleep till it's done"

She had stopped eating
Nothing more to live for
She chose her time of death

✦ ✦ ✦

01.04.2022
I begin to get a glimpse of wholeness
A new self emerging
from scattered parts that rearrange themselves as a motherless child
who knows
she was deeply loved

01.09.2022

Grief has its own agenda
Calling me from distraction at unexpected moments

into awareness of my broken heart
Only tears will do
I succumb again
And again
Each surrendering its
own
fresh
molting
of who I used to be

01.13.2022
Getting to know you all over again
I always knew you weren't your troubles
Relentlessly
You showed up at your new "home"
Such incredible perseverance in your trying
Joy in your newfound friendships
though their names never once landed
even though we repeated them again and again

The only thing that really settled into your brain was your room
You'd tell me about it often, how nice it was
As if I hadn't been the one who—with the fire of love and determination—
made it as beautiful as I could

Now you're free of all that

Giggling with your angels
Here for me like never before
Your own angst and insecurity liberated

The body burned
The crippled brain released
The karmic ties dissolved

I feel your loving presence watching over me so sweetly
Still my heart aches for your voice, your troubles, your hands, your face, the outfits, the telling of your day

Thankful for those moments our hearts connected

Explaining what I meant by certain words that used to be so easy

You wanting to play bridge

The slow understanding of where you were
Not a hotel
A place for old crazy people

You were not sticking around for that

Locked indoors, the beautiful garden below out of reach
They don't want us to go outside, you'd say

All things considered you made the right choice
You got out while you could

Your memory surrounds me
I write with your pen
That's the amethyst I gave you that sat on the dresser in the room I stayed in at your house when I visited
I always loved that candle

And the Saraswati statue
The sculpture I made of a mother holding a baby that sat on the ledge in the hallway
reminds me that your love enfolds me
I look at your photos and see how you loved each of us completely

Damn it, I miss you
I love you
I always did

✦ ✦ ✦

01.14.2022
My mother was on top of her money. She would sit at her desk and pay bills, look at her statements, balance her checkbook. When the numbers became jumbled and confused, she could not face it. So when it was taken away it was the first of a series of devastating losses of independence and the life she knew.
For months in the new place she said she was getting her room for free. There was no use telling her otherwise. If she could have grasped paying $7,000 a month for something she absolutely did not want, she would have. But her brain protected her.

02.01.2022
Ruth Anne, How could you leave like that,
Just give up and go?
A mother is forever
The body I came from
Torn away, now a box of ash
Goodbye, body of my mother
Your five children are changed forever, trying to mend our broken hearts

✦ ✦ ✦

02.02.2022
On the new moon, my guide showed up as Death
face decrepit
flesh rotting
I felt afraid

She showed me a large 3D map
I saw that each person's life is very clearly mapped out

A place where it begins
A place where it ends

Thank you
I now know that my mother lived out her design
in complete perfection

✦ ✦ ✦

11.09.2023
My psyche was immersed in my mother for the last few years of her life as dementia slowly seeped in
Witnessing her mind slowly dying while her heart remained intact and available

The treasure was loving her unconditionally
And being loved in return
When she picked up the phone, "Is this my Susie?"

The unending love is the gift that holds the truth
A mother is forever

22

TWENTY-MINUTE WARNING

Trudy Toliver

Have you ever wondered how you would react if you were told that you would be dead in less than twenty minutes? We all like to believe we would behave honorably, reverently accepting our fate. Although several spiritual workshops had given me a chance to pretend my death and even to dwell on the other side, until faced with that actual situation I didn't know for sure. On January 13, 2018, at around eight in the morning, my husband Michael and I were given the opportunity to learn.

For Michael's birthday, we rented a condo at a seaside golf resort just south of Kona on the Big Island of Hawaii. After a couple of days of swimming, tennis, and too many cocktails, we decided to go exploring. A bright morning sky with occasional puffy clouds, it was a perfect day for a drive and a hike around Hawai'i Volcanoes National Park. We got an early start, packed a supply of water, snacks, and sunscreen, hopped in the rental car, and off we went. The two-hour route would take us south, through small towns, forests, farms, and black lava viewpoints to the Devastation Trail at the park.

After winding our way through the hills, we passed the southernmost point of the island and caught a glimpse of the ocean, but Michael thought the trip was missing something, music. I turned on the radio and began searching for a station that played traditional

Hawaiian music. Scanning the channels, picking up everything but Don Ho, I settled for the local public broadcasting station, when that familiar whirling alarm sound we used to hear from The Emergency Broadcast System began to blare.

I thought, huh, I haven't heard that for decades. I was about to turn the radio off. As I reached for the knob, something unexpected happened. We heard a distant, monotone voice say:

The US Pacific Command has detected a missile threat to Hawaii.

A missile may impact on land or sea within minutes. (Holy shit!)

THIS IS NOT A DRILL. (Oh my God, NOT a drill!)

If you are indoors, stay indoors. If you are outdoors, seek immediate shelter in a building. Remain indoors well away from windows. If you are driving, pull safely to the side of the road and seek shelter in a building or lay on the floor. We will announce when the threat has ended.

THIS IS NOT A DRILL. (OK, this is real)

Take immediate action measures.

At about that same moment, our cell phones alarmed too, something was happening. This message came via text:

Emergency Alert

BALLISTIC MISSILE THREAT INBOUND TO HAWAII,

SEEK IMMEDIATE SHELTER. THIS IS NOT A DRILL.

A government warning! "This is not a drill." Are we suddenly in a dream? I wondered. A chill went through my body and panic crept inside each of us. The words "not a drill" and "take immediate action measures" echoed in my mind but none of the instructions made sense for us. We happened to be amid a miles-wide lava field; there was simply no place to hide. We were blissfully on vacation, I don't think we even had a first aid kit with us, let alone any way to protect ourselves from a bomb.

Michael pulled the car to the shoulder where we stood for a long hug, my body slightly trembling. Swirls of thoughts in our heads, we pondered every alternative. Then, sitting on a low stone retaining wall along the highway with the lava field to our backs and the ocean before us, we voiced what was churning inside us, each with similar thoughts.

"I don't want to die."

"But maybe this really is it, we're at the end of our lives."

"If there is a missile coming toward us, that will be our end."

"I love you, thanks for a great eleven years."

"Maybe we should call home."

I wanted to call my mom, but her dementia had reached the middle stage by then. It just did not seem right to frighten and confuse her. I called my cousin, knowing he could handle the news and to find out if he'd heard if it was true. Mike called a friend whose wife is in the Air Force, for similar reasons. After a few more calls in our dazed state of uncertainty, we decided to continue down the road to see if we could reach the volcano before the missile reached us.

As we chatted, we envisioned that the "missile" would wreak complete annihilation upon us, vaporized, Hiroshima-style. Even if there was a place for us to shelter, it seemed a useless chore. As logic entered our minds, Michael guessed the missile's target to be Pearl Harbor, many miles away so there may be a chance to see the explosion coming toward us.

"If that happens," he said, "we should be holding hands." Perhaps our vision of quick obliteration eased our fears. No pain, no suffering, just immediate death, freedom from these bodies. Were we fools?

We drove some more, sharing how grateful we each were for the lives we led, how happy we've been together, and that we had no regrets. Sure, life dealt us ups and downs, more ups for me and more downs for him, but we agreed that life had been fun, interesting, and satisfying. We were pleased that we held similar core beliefs about how life works. When we considered the big picture, that we were just tiny wiggling specks stuck on a bigger rocky speck floating in a vast void of black space, we each felt perfectly comfortable dying. What a precious gift we were given, the opportunity to consider and accept this destiny.

About twenty minutes after our calls home, my cousin phoned back to say the national news reported that it was a false alarm. But we couldn't absorb that information, we couldn't believe it. We had settled, maybe desperately, into what we thought was our fate. Our hearts and minds had made sense of that reality.

Finally, about forty minutes after the first alert, the cell phones and radio emergency services broadcast rang out again.

"False alarm."

"What?" I gasped. Emotionally spent, even with the preview from my cousin, I couldn't quickly shift again. I couldn't accept that my willingness to let life go was purposeless. We sat in denial of the whole thing for several silent minutes. Then stopped the car again for a long hug and to recover our breath. Still somewhat dazed, we eventually continued toward the fiery, bubbling volcano.

Tears come again every time I relive that hour of my life. It's more than a memory. It returns that deep sense of connection and relief that came when I believed that soon I'd draw my last breath. Maybe that's what a profound spiritual experience is. I stood willing to give my life away to a pending catastrophe, unattached to the fear of what may come.

I've studied yoga for more than twenty-five years. Commonly, during a yoga class, we are asked to surrender, so I have practiced it many times. My master yoga teacher describes savasana (the resting pose at the end of class) as "dying before you die," and then suggests that we surrender to the all-knowing. So, I slowly exhale to loosen my muscles' grip on my bones. Another profound rehearsal of dying before I die was during an Andean mysticism training in Peru. We stood among ancient stone ruins placed by the Inca on a hillside overlooking a sweeping valley outside of Cusco. Our Peruvian teacher guided us through a meditation stepping us slowly toward our death, then over the threshold. Literally, he asked us to lift a foot up and over an imaginary low rock wall. I dwelt there on the other side cautious at first but soon I felt safe, and I relaxed into the peace of this heavenly place in my mind. Like others in that group, I did not want to come back. The other side felt so spacious, unfettered, and sweet.

These esoteric practices of release, acceptance, and joy prepared me to surrender my physical life. This day was my real-life chance to open the doorways to a higher power; to feel so free, I wish I could fly with it again and again. I wish we could all die fully cognizant of our last few minutes. That bit of time allows us to say goodbye, to briefly recount life, and to be endlessly grateful for everything.

Today, I share this story not as a defining but as a confirming moment, a validation point experience. When I was fourteen my parents divorced, and my mom sought comfort at a nearby Unity Church. I joined her for some personal development workshops. One crystal clear memory of that time is an exercise we did about making amends and avoiding regrets. I vowed then to live without regrets. My young self was determined to honor those beliefs.

Holding the intention to live without regret and practicing letting go when it is time allowed me to get through my "this is not a drill moment." I kept in mind that my life is just a fragment of the whole. Surrendering to the energy of the universe is a sacred value in the practice of yoga. So, I'll continue to practice surrender in savasana at the end of each class, ready for my truly final exhale.

23

THIS BAFFLING, BEAUTIFUL LIFE

Jennifer Golbus

If I close my eyes, I can bring myself back in an instant to what it was like before the miracle. I can remember the self-loathing. The shame. The burning of the tears. And I can feel the despair—that unique mixture of sadness, anger, and desperation that used to consume me in the darkness of my addiction.

I always loved the effect alcohol had on me. I loved the anticipation of that first sip of crisp, cold elixir sliding down my throat while simultaneously easing into my brain to provide instant relief. "Relax!" it would demand, and I happily obeyed.

I chose a brilliant career for a budding alcoholic, doing publicity for high-end wineries located near my hometown in Northern California. I felt so sophisticated in my twenties, dressing in my nice suits, interviewing winemakers, walking the vineyards, writing vineyard profiles and fancy brochures, and planning elaborate press events. The glamour of it all was intoxicating. In came the bespoke glasses specifically crafted for each type of wine, the specialized refrigerator to keep wines at just the right temperature, the wine racks, and all of the wine paraphernalia. It was a lifestyle, and I loved it.

In a culture where fine wine is celebrated, home chefs pride themselves on pairing their culinary creations with the perfect pinot noir, and chardonnay is on display in the produce section of grocery stores, I never thought twice about my drinking. It was effortless to tell myself that I drank like everyone else. That everyone anticipated that first sip of relief awaiting them when they arrived home from work. That cracking a second bottle on a Tuesday evening was totally the norm—just to have one extra half-glass of that delicious Bordeaux blend from my new client, of course. That it was normal to wake up every day with a headache and cotton between my ears, which was cleared only with the first sip the following evening. It's just what people did.

But did "people" also yell at themselves in the mirror, chastising themselves to get their shit together, to try harder, to be a good person?

In the world of recovery, we assert, "We do not regret the past nor wish to shut the door on it." As a mother who drank, this was the most difficult aspiration on my windy road to recovery.

Let's flash forward to the day. The day when I crashed my car into a parked vehicle on my way to pick up my four-year-old twins from preschool. Looking back now, I can see what a blessing the accident was. I shudder to think what might have happened if I had made it to the preschool that afternoon and buckled my children into their car seats. How does a mother ever hold her head high again, after knowing she put her children in such danger? How do I?

When I first began my journey into the world of recovery, I remember people saying, "You never have to drink again."

As if that was some kind of consolation. Maybe they didn't know they were talking to someone who could scarcely leave the house without the armor of alcohol flowing in her veins. I wanted to scream, "Fuck you! I WANT to drink!" Instead, I politely nodded.

I thought they were all lying. I didn't believe they got through entire days without so much as a sip—it was completely beyond my comprehension. Just a few hours dry, and I would be crawling out of my skin, so uncomfortable that merely existing felt unbearable at times. I was at the jumping-off point. I knew I couldn't live without alcohol, and I knew I had to learn to do just that.

Getting sober is hands down the hardest thing I have ever done. It's also the most rewarding. But of course, I did not know that back then. When you fall asleep every night and wake up every morning crying, it can be hard to see the blessing.

So, how did I get his way? How did a girl who attended private high school, graduated from UCLA, and started her own company in her twenties become such a colossal mess? The AA "Big Book" warns, "Remember that we deal with alcohol—cunning, baffling and powerful." I find these three adjectives to be spot on.

Cunning. It's smarter than I am. It whispers to me in my own voice, telling me to pop in at the grocery store to buy butter so that I can demonstrate my love for my children with from-scratch chocolate chip cookies when, what it really wants is to get me to the store so that I see those mouth-watering displays of chardonnay and walk out with a bottle.

Baffling. The very definition of having no idea what is happening to you, and why, despite your ability to achieve everything else in the course of your life that you have ever set your mind to, including swimming the length of the Golden Gate Bridge, teaching a class on the Holocaust to peers in high school, and starting a thriving business during a recession, why you are utterly incapable of stopping the insanity, even though you are destroying your life and putting your children in danger.

Powerful. This thing is so powerful that not even the love of a mother for her children is strong enough to defeat it. This brutal truth was such a blow to my identity as a mother, it took me years to move through the shame and forgive myself.

The incomprehensible demoralization that so many alcoholics speak of happened to me as a member of AA. For three and a half years, I relapsed. I stayed sober for three weeks, four months, and even six months at one point. Then I drank. I would return the next day, resolving to dig deeper for the willingness to begin again. And again. And again. I shared in meetings, I met with my sponsor each week, and I did my step work. I went to therapy. I tried hypnosis. I prayed. I reached out to others in the program. And still, I drank.

I remember the look in my husband's eyes the day he came home from work after a sober spell, to find me drunk in the kitchen, with our young children running amok, attempting to cook dinner. His was a look of utter sadness and disappointment, and it chilled me to my core. And yet. I drank again.

I began to lose hope. I believed that perhaps I was one of those unfortunate people for whom sobriety would remain elusive. I watched the whispers of my husband with his parents through the kitchen window and understood he might leave me. I pictured myself living alone in an apartment with visitation rights for my own children, who were the sunlight of my existence, and I knew I wouldn't want to live if that became my reality. And yet. And yet. I drank. This is the definition of desperation and insanity. It was all-consuming, and it was terrifying.

When I finally became willing to truly surrender and follow in the footsteps of those who have walked before me, nothing short of a miracle followed.

And now …

"Dear Mom, I am so proud to be your daughter. I am so grateful you are a part of my life. You are a role model and inspire others. Thank you for showing me change is possible if you believe in yourself!"

"You cannot imagine how much your listening ear and support means to me. I'm very protective of my privacy but my walls with you come down. I am so blessed to have you in my life. You are a bracha (blessing) to our family." My sister-in-law.

"I feel blessed to know you." A colleague.

The completeness of the transformation into the woman I was always meant to be still stuns me at times.

Another gift was revealed a year or two into my journey. I have proudly identified as a Jew all my life and have strived for spiritual connection as a Jew. When I got sober and began living on a spiritual basis, my Jewish experience grew deeper. Suddenly I had a personal relationship with the God that was in my Jewish prayers. At first, my Jewish identity made me feel like an outsider in AA because I perceived Christian undertones in the volume Alcoholics Anonymous (otherwise known as "The Big Book"), which contains the blueprint for the twelve-step program of recovery. But once I learned to look for the similarities, I was surprised to see my Jewish prayer book come alive as AA prayers, and my AA prayers suddenly felt Jewish. Over time, I realized that the spiritual path I was walking in my recovery was one and the same as the spiritual path that was beginning to open up to me in my Jewish world.

One of my favorite Jewish prayers is the Modeh Ani—a morning gratitude prayer. Imagine that our souls leave our bodies at night and go to be recharged while we're sleeping. Each morning, God makes a decision to return our souls to our bodies, so the first thing we do when we wake up is to thank God for one more day of life. With that responsibility, I am to go out into the world and shine God's light. What a beautiful thought.

Today, people tell me I am the "queen of good vibes." They come to me for advice. I am a trustworthy friend. My clients depend on my counsel. I have rebuilt trust in my marriage. I dance in my kitchen. I give back to my community. I watch other people's kids for them when they go out of town. I find humor in almost everything. Who knew that sober laughing was the very best kind? The tears-rolling-down-your-cheeks, pee-in-your-pants kind that heals most of what ails you? That discovery remains one of my favorite gifts of recovery.

Each morning my first thought when I wake up is, "Thank you for another day." I barely recognize the woman who used to wake up crying. Thank God, she is a distant memory. Today I feel joy, contentment, and happiness. I also feel stress, disappointment, and uncertainty—I just don't drink over those uncomfortable feelings anymore, and I have come to embrace it all as the wonderful, messy blessing of being human.

The volume Alcoholics Anonymous says, "Making a decision to look for the good in our experiences and in our friends and acquaintances frees us from so much frustration. It ushers in happiness, not only for us but for others we are treating agreeably. Happiness is a by-product of living the right kind of life."

I love that happiness as a sober, dignified woman is the natural by-product of how I choose to live, not the result of my accomplishments, my belongings, or where I go on vacation. I love that today, the solution often has nothing to do with the problem, and that it almost always is about doing something beyond myself, bringing happiness to another. Today, I know that even when life doesn't feel happy, it is always a blessing. I know that I am loved, and that I am capable of giving love. I know that when things get hard, this too shall pass, and I search for the hidden gifts.

When I first began my sobriety journey, I would cry in desperation, mortified that I simply could not stop drinking even for the sake of my children. But doing the work of recovery cleared away the cobwebs of my destructive thinking and behavior so that light could shine through.

Today, when I practice forgiveness, take responsibility for my actions, and strive to live right, I feel connection and intuition, which I have come to understand as God, The Universe, Source Energy, or whatever you would like to call it. Today I'm willing to choose how I act instead of acting how I feel. I pray for strength to walk through what is happening instead of praying for things to turn out my way. I strive to live without anger, resentment, self-pity, and fear. I reach for connection and seek to bring something to the world each day I am blessed with being here.

24
WHY WE HATE HOUSEWORK

Helen Hayward

"Living an artful life means accepting the need to do the work that supports this ideal." — Jenny Willie

When I sat down with Jenny Willie, to talk about her domestic life, and she spoke these words to me, they immediately rang true. Because by this point in my life, I'd embraced the work that underlies a warm and pleasant home. Among my other roles, I too, was a housekeeper.

If I thought my struggle with housekeeping was mine alone, I'd have given up studying it long ago. However, talking to scores of people about their homes, over these last ten years, has made me realize that pretty much everyone struggles with caring for themselves, where they live, and the people they love most—with what I call home work.

Of all the findings that arose from these conversations, this is perhaps the biggest: The more we were loved and cared for as children, the more we struggle with housekeeping once we grow up. This appears counterintuitive. Surely if we were well looked after as kids, we'd have housekeeping modeled for us in a way that makes taking over the reins ourselves no big deal. We wouldn't go on to resist household tasks. We wouldn't bicker about who does what. We'd find time to be creative at home. We'd just get on with it. Yet so often we don't. Why not?

When we were small, the practicalities of daily life were taken out of our hands. Our shoes were slipped on and our jacket zipped up. We weren't expected to pack our own lunch on the first day of school. We took it for granted that someone else would do these things for us.

As a girl, my parents gave my sisters and me rotating chores—setting the table, feeding the animals, and emptying the bins—and docked our pocket money if we forgot. But doing weekly chores in no way prepared me for the shock of moving into a share-house where no one picked up the slack after me. When I look back on moving out of home, I see a loss of innocence. Overnight, I was forced to give up my carefreeness, my carelessness. I felt pressures that, in my childhood home, I had no inkling of.

But it was only when I moved solo into a studio flat that my real training in home work began. Every day I was learning on the job. And it wasn't just practicalities. I was learning how to hold space for myself, as much as I was learning how much fluff under the bed and yuk in the fridge I could bear. I was discovering how much my ability to hold space for myself—to make the place where I lived feel like home—was tied to my willingness to embrace domesticity as integral to my life.

I made this discovery before I had a family. But it wasn't until my second child was born that my domestic DNA came to the surface. Being a mother of two children made me more conscientious in my housekeeping. I wasn't compulsive, but I was definitely organized. I was keen to head off meltdowns. I did give a thought to the following night's dinner before flicking off the kitchen light and heading to bed. Also, I was married to a man who considered me provincial because in his mind I cared about things that, given his bohemian upbringing and Oxford education, didn't really matter.

During these early years of family life, I took my domestic struggles personally. It's not that I thought other people were spared them. I just assumed that everyone I knew must feel them less acutely because, if they didn't, they'd draw more attention to them.

It was only when my kids became teenagers that I had enough time, energy, and space to develop my thoughts about the home. Nowhere—in all my reading of Sigmund Freud, Carl Jung, Pierre Janet, Karen Horney, Melanie Klein, Honoré Balzac, the Brontes, George Eliot, and Tolstoy—did I find an intelligent, rounded discussion of domesticity.

There were mentions of it here and there, but mostly as a symptom or plot entanglement. It wasn't ignored altogether. It wasn't left out exactly. I just never came across a sustained and full description of it. I never found an adequate explanation of why conversations about cleaning and cooking and laundry and renovating and gardening and hobbies and DIY and household budgets and real estate provoked such electric reactions in people.

Nothing shed light on why I might have one friend who waxed lyrical about making orange marmalade late at night and another who went into paroxysms over mopping the kitchen floor.

"Pushing wet mush around the floor," he said, almost spitting, "it makes my skin crawl."

It was only after I sat down for fifty conversations with people about their home life that the penny dropped. Only then did I realize that the more we were loved and cared for as children, the more we struggle with housekeeping as adults. How can this be true?

My hunch is that the better our needs and demands were met as kids, the more outrageous it is to us, as grown-ups, that we must satisfy our needs and demands ourselves.

But do we tantrum? Mostly we don't. We keep quiet about this outrage. Reasonable creatures that we are, whenever our hot and messy domestic feelings are triggered, we smother them. We keep a lid on them. We refuse to admit that in fantasy—and in our unconscious—when anything domestic does come up, it's at the hands of someone else. (Not by chance is Harry Potter's boarding school, Hogwarts, maintained by house elves who magically whisk in and out of rooms.)

Here on Planet Earth, we're destined to look after ourselves. So unpalatable is this truth—in fantasy, this error—that we deflect it onto the people we love and/or live with. It's our partner who makes outrageous demands on us, not ourselves. Perhaps it's our child or neighbor. We, meanwhile, are mature adults who take pride in keeping abreast of the demands that home life makes on us.

In some ways, our relationship to home is just as important as our relationship with the people we live with and/or care about most. Our home isn't animate. It doesn't talk back to us. But while it isn't a companion as such, most of us are in a fairly constant dialogue with it. Our home has needs and desires that we can neither fully ignore nor fully satisfy. It's full of objects and unfinished projects that make a demand on our attention each time we brush past them. With each passing day, a layer of dust falls over every surface. Dust that, to preserve our sanity, we fail to notice. Instead, our attention is drawn to finger marks on cupboard doors, leaves heaped in corners after a storm, or pet hair speckling car seats.

Unless we outsource all our household tasks, travel continuously, or have a dysfunctional relationship with a compliant partner, none of us escapes the joys and sorrows of house work. But then why would we want to anyway? What a mistake that would be.

"Society doesn't care about how we spend our free time," said Helen Mirren, "which makes it all the more important that we find our own private Netherlands."

Because it's when we're at home that we get to let down our guard, explore parts of ourselves that we haven't found a place for in the world, and to try new things.

When the story we tell ourselves about home is that of endless chores and streamed entertainment, we lose sight of its promise. We end up talking more about our frustrations, the things we don't or can't do, than about our satisfaction with the things we can do. We overlook the beauty and calm that is ours after completing the housework for the week. We forget how the chatter mellows around the table after a meal with friends. We gloss over the pride that finishing a craft project gives us. And yet these feelings of contentment are real. Just as real as our frustrations with washing up and laundry.

When we treat the work we do at home as a practice, rather than a forlorn parade of tasks that in fantasy really should be done by someone else, feeling content at home can be ours again and again. Feeling content with who we are and what we have and what we do at home becomes our new normal.

This is why it's so important that we cultivate a good relationship with home. The kind of relationship that supplies us with enough courage and energy to do things at home that make our spirit sing. The kind of relationship that doesn't heckle us with musts and shoulds and if onlys. The kind of relationship that, when we leave home and come back again, we see it with fresh eyes. The kind of relationship that encourages us, through our own creativity, to keep a childlike, irresponsible part of ourselves alive.

Few of us conquer our struggles with home life. It doesn't matter how many weeks, years, or decades we've looked after ourselves for, we all live close to the edge. At any moment we can tip into feeling overwhelmed. We're never fully in control. There are too many factors, our lives are too complex for serenity and calm. Likewise our triumphs—a clean pantry, a big dinner, a spring-cleaned flat—are temporary. Thankfully there is a big consolation. Which is that everyone shares in this struggle. Partnered or not, children or not, we all wrestle with the sea monster that lives beneath the surface of our relatively well-run lives.

This makes it essential that we celebrate our small wins. Those moments when, after accomplishing whatever it is, we feel in our bones that a pleasant home is worth striving for, and that by investing our love, time, and energy into it we're passing on a way of life that may be of value to generations to come.

"Nothing is so bad that there's no good in it." This Finnish saying captures what I'm getting at. Once we put aside our evaluative lens, our judginess—around good and bad, right and wrong, fair and unfair, beautiful and disgusting, time well spent and time wasted—and view our home life just as it is, the pressure lifts. As if by magic, feeling content at home becomes possible. By treating housekeeping as a practice, as a means to a good and sometimes meaningful life, simply by taking the next right step, by doing the next right thing, our home is there to give back to us.

"There is something empowering about learning how to take care of your own space," writes Melissa Maker, a professional cleaner. "When you live in a space and look after it, you feel better about it."

25

FREEZE. YELL. SING.

Tessa Lynne Alburn

FREEZE. Tonight, lying on my sofa … unsure of the words to put on paper like so many writers until that moment that pen goes to paper, I am uncertain for a few more moments the story I will share.

Instead, I call in Reiki life force energy and begin my needed healing routine.

Hmm. Strange … Nothing, it seems. My hands aren't even warm today. I move through the sequence, landing on the spot around my throat. A thought of letting go of perfectionism to write my story moves across the screen of my mind and … WHAM! Shaking. Tears. A brief release of some traumas past.

As a young girl who was terrified to exist, I moved from one disassociated moment to the next, escaping my body whenever possible to avoid the potential hurt or abuse that could befall me at any moment …. Looking back, I see now I was in a pickle—or as therapists now call it, a "double bind."

I am descended from a line of exceedingly talented musicians, including my grandmother, who may have been one of the most phenomenal organists in the Northern Hemisphere. Ascribed to a life of poverty following her divorce in the mid-'60s, she lived to age sixty-five in a sandy, barren trailer park about ten miles from us, up old US 101, teaching piano to ungrateful teens.

She seemed an odd character to my sister and me, and certainly unlikely to play the organ at a mere five feet two inches or so in height. But her hands and legs connected with the five octaves of keys and pedals like an Irish leprechaun celebrating her pot of gold on the way to heaven's pub.

Last week I turned sixty-five, so I suppose that somehow, it's fitting that my grandmother comes to mind in connection with this personal tale.

Yet it was mostly my mother's influence that shaped my fears and inability to perform.

"Sing, dammit!" I hear the faint echo of her voice, knowing she meant well—but of course it didn't land that way with me. As a child, it felt dangerous and unsafe.

My mother was a church choir director, who had a knack for getting others to sing. But for some reason, she couldn't get me to. I knew that she desperately wanted to show me off. She rehearsed and prodded me, all the while expressing her exasperation, to no avail. The moment I was in the presence of others, terror gripped me. Not a single note squeaked out.

Silence.

Ah! The vortex opens and tears leak down my face. I'm frozen and hot at the same time. I don't know what she wants from me. I don't know how to be perfect.

Fragile perfection is frozen deep inside of me, and I can't let it out. I dare not let it out.

By the time I was eight years old, I had a well-developed fear of annihilation. I had learned I could be destroyed if my voice gave way to discontent, God forbid a tantrum, or simply asking for something I wanted or needed. I could be sent to a place of darkness and pain. I had been taught that my voice could betray me.

I learned my lesson well. True or not, the only way I felt I could speak was to be "perfect." To bring home perfect grades and never ever speak up. So I learned at a very early age to conform and keep myself intact by running to avoid. Avoiding any number of encounters with a four-inch black belt and staying away from home for hours at a time. Until things cooled off, I hoped.

YELL. In 2010, I attended a women's facilitator training program. On the drive to the beach site, the facilitator began to purposefully trigger me by firing questions at me, intentionally designed to push me so I could confront my own long-held beliefs about who I was.

"You created that! Why would you create that?" she pointedly challenged.

I was stunned by her direct confrontation and suddenly felt like a small animal needing to defend its turf from the back seat of the van. I had no words, and nowhere to go. Though the thought crossed my mind, I couldn't just jump out of a moving vehicle.

Immediately, I experienced an overwhelming, hot rush of fear. My adult brain went offline, and then the old instinct deep within activated fully as my inner systems began to rapidly shut down—my brain, my body, and my emotions.

"Tessa, shut it down, now! Stop being so sensitive! Get a grip!" My inner critic wrenched me back under its control.

Two seconds later, I was in Freeze, while squelching the rage running through me. Unable to breathe and at the same time, seeing red.

How dare she tell me I created that mess in my life?! How dare she tell me I created myself as a victim? I was incredulous; somehow having a new set of sensations and emotions layered onto Freeze.

Upon arrival at our coastal destination, I pushed my enraged feelings aside and waited for the others to clear out of the van before I moved an inch.

Silently slipping out of the van, I observed our location. We were at an extraordinarily rugged and dynamic lava beach, with water crashing upon jagged rocks and spraying out all over the slick black forms beneath our feet.

As I looked out toward the ocean and its dynamism I spied a trapped pool of tidal seawater, held back by the walls of lava, spread out and shallow akin to a kiddie pool.

The process instructions were simple: Find a place to journal and release something that was holding us back in our current life situation. For me, that meant releasing something that was holding me back from being empowered, releasing the thing that was keeping me from being fully seen and authentic.

Still shaking with fear and anger, I gingerly walked the shallow tide pool, seeking refuge in its unmoving waters and making ineffectual attempts to soothe myself. I wanted to cry—I felt so very betrayed. Betrayed by my feelings of anger while also feeling betrayed by the facilitator who I thought was there to support me. Uncertain where to sit and journal, I carefully avoided eye contact with the other women in the group, so no one could glimpse my weakness or rage. As I silently prayed for a breakthrough of some kind that could change my life direction, I spiraled full tilt into a pool of despondency.

Stew, stew, doubt, doubt, crush the self.

Time passed.

Eventually, even in my mostly shut-down state, I became aware that I was one of two women who had not yet completed the assignment given. The others were back in the vans, awaiting our breakthroughs. Ahhh! I did not want to be the one who can't get it, who doesn't get her breakthrough!

So there I was, too afraid to do anything, too afraid not to. Wandering around still in a frenzy of silent anger, not having any idea what to do about it except hope and pray this, too, would pass.

I left the tide pool and moved up to the wet black rock, finding something I could sit upon for two minutes without adding physical pain into the mix.

The facilitator sidled up to me. I braced and took a breath, then closed my eyes.

"You are urgent," she said. She repeated the words once more as they pounded through me like sledgehammers on clay, smooshing my cells and simultaneously reverberating loudly. "You are urgent," she repeated.

I gasped and wept as I felt her love.

She stepped back to continue to hold the sacred space.

I wept some more, releasing tears out to the sea as the ocean sprayed over me. As I cried, something began to build inside me. Something I had no recollection of having felt before … a sense of power. And then, I knew I needed to scream. To give this new feeling a voice.

After wrestling with that idea for a few minutes more, I did just that.

I took a big breath and with terrified might, let forth a long, intense scream, "Aaaaaaaaaaaahhhhhhhhhhhhhh!"

The other formerly silent woman in the group jumped up and began to scream with me. We screamed and screamed, each scream lengthening beyond our known capacities, until finally, our screams turned into yells of power as we tribally urged the other on. I started to feel the power of hearing my own voice. The power of letting

Mother Nature witness me and heal my pain. And in that moment, I transmuted a lifetime of silence into an ocean's roar.

I was liberated. Unbound.

This was my soul coming forth to have her voice.

And now, this is part of my way.

When I need to connect and am unable to do so, I stand in my power and open my throat and shout to the mountains or the sea.

"No more silence!"

"I need your support!"

"Show me, Creator! Show me, Soul!"

"I need you NOW!"

And she comes. Soul always does.

SING. As a finally liberated woman, I now enjoy karaoke, rock and roll, and screaming out Janis Joplin songs with my sometimes wild, yet angelic voice. And I even show up when I'm scared that I'll be too messy or sting someone's feelings harshly with my Scorpio tongue. Thank you, dear Soul. I am grateful you are mine and we get to sing and moan and yell and create magic.

We are alive.

26

THE POWER OF REST

Cindi Buenzli Gertz

Rest saved my life. You might think that as a yoga teacher, I'd say, "Yoga saved me." But no, I credit rest with liberating my life and allowing me to gracefully navigate the messy in-between we call midlife.

When I wrote this story, I had just turned fifty and crossed the threshold of menopause. In the same year, we had packed our son off to college another state away and taught our daughter how to drive—transitions that nudged us closer to the empty nest.

But I would not go quietly into the next chapter of my life. I celebrated these milestones not with a sense of dread, but rather enthusiasm. I felt healthier and more vibrant than ever, full of joy, wonder, gratitude, abundance, and excitement for the future. As I danced through the mystery of menopause, I felt ready to expand, grow, and imagine possibilities for the second half of my life.

In my younger years, however, vibrancy eluded me. Fresh out of college, I veered toward burnout with breakneck speed. I came from a family rooted in an unhealthy work ethic. I paid for college on my own, took a full course load, and often held multiple jobs at a time to make ends meet.

When I graduated, I headed into the nonprofit world to make a difference. And I kept right on working—pushing, pleasing, and perfecting through the first years of my professional life. I skimped on my self-care in every way and saw zero value in taking breaks and getting rest.

My mind always moved and so did my body—like a machine. I forgot to maintain the sacred vessel housing my soul. I refused to hit the off switch. I took care of everyone else. While I spent seven years employed by major nonprofits, I kept saying "yes" to work. And "no" to me.

I developed seasonal affective disorder (SAD) at the age of twenty-eight. I started to fumble, barely able to get out of bed and to work on time. I endured horrific headaches from carrying my work stress to bed with me.

Chronic seasonal allergies worsened and left my immune system on overdrive and completely weakened. As a result, I experienced repeated colds. Starting in late summer, they raged on for months until I developed a full-blown sinus infection by the holidays. This cycle went on for years.

Still, I kept pushing. Until my body screamed—"enough!"

On a 1999 work trip, I found myself stuck at the Detroit Airport after a blizzard grounded all planes. Foolishly, I thought it brilliant to rent a car with two college students and drive back home, a ten-hour journey in good weather.

My wake-up call came the day after I survived that unbelievable trip. As I stood in our local grocery store looking at the cans of processed soup, the world closed in on me. The edges of my vision started turning black, the light withdrew into a small circle, and … I woke up in the middle of the canned goods aisle.

Fortunately, my brother had been standing right next to me. He carried me to the bench at the front of the store. The urgent care doctor we saw that afternoon put me on a week of bed rest.

Around the time of my wake-up call, a volunteer I was working with suggested I try yoga. I can still remember the relief I felt when my teacher told me I could rest and let go. Tears leaked from my eyes as I lay on my mat for the first time.

That day she gave me permission to rest, but years passed before I would grant myself that same grace. Relaxing, resting, and just "being" were the hardest parts of yoga for me to learn. I almost gave up on yoga during my first year of practice.

Still newlyweds, my husband and I were wrapped up in the details of moving to a new town, renting our first house, and starting new jobs.

I came home one day completely overwhelmed and sighed, "I'm too busy. I don't have time for yoga right now."

He replied, "Honey, don't you know that's when you need it the most?"

That moment sank in. I recommitted to finding a teacher in my new town, and the very next week, she walked into my office. She introduced herself to me and said she was looking for a new yoga studio space. And once again, yoga found me.

After a year, she invited me to consider teacher training so that I could help her out with the growing yoga community. In 2002, I attended Kripalu Center for Yoga and Health and earned my teacher certificate. At that point, I had no idea the changes that would take place in my life.

The next year, we moved to another state, bought our first home, and grew our family to four. I juggled managing our home with caring for kids and pets, homeschooling, and volunteering. I also opened my first yoga studio.

Crazy busy again, my body howled. I landed in the ER doubled over with abdominal pain. A large cyst had formed in my pelvic cavity. Surgery was suggested, but this time, I listened to my body. I turned to my yoga tools.

I had recently fallen in LOVE with restorative yoga. Yoga props gently held and supported me in poses that helped me release tension and renew my energy. I took a holistic approach, combining restorative and intuitive practices that allowed me to heal without surgery.

Soon after, I jumped at the chance to earn my Relax & Renew Teacher Certificate. Then, I began teaching restorative yoga to other women who had also burned out and broken down. While guiding these women, I deepened my own practice of rest and relaxation. My awakening slowly continued to unfold.

And the shifts have been enormous. In years past, I measured the health of my moods and the intensity of my SAD by how many days I just wanted to crawl back into bed and bury my head under the covers. I felt drawn toward this abyss most days. These days, depression no longer threatens to drag me under.

I still get the occasional headache, but now I have tools to help. I barely notice my allergies anymore. I can breathe freely and easily and have energy for my everyday activities. I no longer get colds that last for weeks on end. If I get one, maybe two a year, they last three to five days at most. And I haven't had a sinus infection since 2003.

Probably the most profound impact of rest came during my perimenopause journey, which lasted more than ten years. I went through the ups and downs of perimenopause like most women. Then came a time when my hot flashes surged. Night sweats drenched me. Sleep-deprived, I felt foggy-brained and bobble-headed for days. I was exhausted. But I didn't suffer. Instead, I rested. I practiced restorative yoga every day. With a little encouragement from friends, I took a six-month sabbatical.

I realize not every woman has the means to take a long break. So, I'm dedicated to teaching women how to take mini sabbaticals during their days. I'll teach restorative yoga to every woman who will give herself permission to pause. If she can't give herself permission yet, I hold that belief for her until she can.

During my sabbatical, I became very still. I put the call out to the divine feminine to guide me. I invited in her presence. Then, I waited and listened. I awakened to her song and the scene she painted for me.

I saw vividly, a circle of women swirling around in my mind. I recalled a dream I'd had years before that suddenly made complete sense. Early in my marriage, I had dreamed of a symbol, what appeared to be a flower. Glowing in hues of burnt orange, tangerine and coral, the petals folded around each other reminding me of the shape of the vulva, or the yoni. At that time, when I awoke from the dream, I drew a picture of it that I still have.

I also heard "start a circle of women who can go through perimenopause together." I felt the idea of a sisterhood of celebration, a new legacy rising up—one that could break the silence around the most potent but undervalued and overlooked time of a woman's life. I wanted to lean into, not push away, this rite of passage.

Now, I'm a midlife midwife. I bring the divine feminine into my sisters' yoga and self-care practices. They, in turn, bring it into their relationships, their work, and their lives. I help them navigate the unknowns and anxiety of midlife with more ease, calm, grace, and confidence. I help them birth themselves into the next iteration of who they're becoming.

And it's magical. Countless times, I've said to students, "There's no magic pill or fix. The magic's IN the practice."

I've asked myself why it took me so long to find that magic? I believe my perception of time got in the way. The mantra "I don't have enough time" ran through my head constantly. I had lived in scarcity mode for years and heard repeatedly from myself and other women what I call the "Four Not Enoughs":

- not enough time
- not enough energy
- not enough money
- and every variation of I'm not enough

Here's the secret I didn't know back then: Every time I practiced restorative yoga, I shattered another limiting belief around the scarcity mentality. I replaced my mindset with one of abundance.

By the time we women reach midlife, we've become expert doers, and we're depleted. Restorative yoga offers rest and renewal. One doesn't do restorative yoga; one receives restorative yoga. Every time I rest, I fill up my well of being.

Years ago, I discovered why rest is so very important for the midlife woman. I realized that most women, me included, engage in two key behaviors that keep their needs on the back burner.

Women are really good at holding the bigger picture for their families and taking this view into account with every decision they make. Women also anticipate the needs of everyone else around them, unfortunately at the cost of foreseeing their own desires.

Every woman likely requires a whole lot more rest than she's getting. More rest than she thinks she needs. And worse yet, more than she thinks she deserves.

A great paradox puzzles me. The stage of life when a woman needs the most rest coincides exactly with the time she is least able to make space for it. Women in midlife are sandwiched between raising children, reaching the height of a career, managing a home, volunteering in their communities, and caring for aging parents.

Then, perimenopause arrives. No wonder so many women lament there isn't any time for them.

Resting taught me not to push away, push down, or push through. It helped me move through midlife and into menopause more peacefully. As I sank into my restorative yoga props, relief washing over me, I leaned into the "pause" in perimenopause.

I invite you to do the same. Savor this time. Bathe in it; soak in it. Let the creative juices of your waning menstrual flow move in new directions allowing you to manifest the body, being, and life you desire most. Let yourself wonder and dream.

Remember my dream of the flower? I contemplated that mystical symbol for years. I finally realized the image represented my own and every woman's awakening and unfolding. The divine feminine awoke my receptivity, intuition, and trust. I remembered to listen to my inner wisdom.

I help my clients understand that they hold the power and that they alone hold the key to saying yes to themselves. I provide the space and the guidance, and like my teacher did for me so many years ago, I offer permission to rest. Nothing will miraculously change to create the space that anyone needs for self-care practices, but with grace, we realize that the magic is in the practice.

27

TAKING THE LEAP ... AND BACK AGAIN

Angie Byas

I am a lawyer by trade and education. Commercial real estate mostly, nothing too sexy or interesting. Definitely no courtroom drama for me. I was drawn to this profession as a young woman with a bachelor's degree in English and no job prospects in sight, so I figured, how could I go wrong with a career built on research and writing? What I didn't know then—about the profession or about myself—would take years to make any sense.

Real-life courtroom dramas are some of my favorite TV shows to watch. I am hooked on true crime stories like Dateline and 20/20. It is very intriguing to watch these attorneys present their case like they are writing an epic story. When they do it well, it is brilliant to watch. But most people picture a lawyer's work like a scene from Ally McBeal. Beautiful young lawyers in fashionable suits and high heels, sitting around a conference table or arguing their case before a judge. In truth, very little time is spent inside the courtroom. Numerous people have told me over the years that I'm not actually a "real" lawyer because I never go to court. That's how little most people understand about my profession.

To me, being a lawyer often feels like a no-holds-barred wrestling match where opponents try to outmaneuver each other in every possible way. Which one is the smartest or best in class? Who is willing to sacrifice their lifestyle and work the longest hours? Who can bully the other into submission during a negotiation? This may be an exaggeration, but it's how I felt every day for twenty years. It requires a strong ego and supreme confidence. And if you don't have those things, you learn to fake it so you don't get swallowed whole. After some time, I lost a sense of which parts of me were real and which ones were a part I was playing at work.

It took me a while to land my first job after law school. When I finally got an offer from a small local firm, I was over the moon. It did wonders for my confidence because they were willing to take a chance on me. I quickly recognized that much of what I learned in law school was theoretical and what I was missing was on-the-job skills. I struggled from day one. The older paralegals had more experience, and frankly, more knowledge than I did. I walked around feeling like an imposter, but I didn't have enough self-awareness yet to understand it. Wasn't I supposed to know how to be a lawyer? Weren't they just supposed to take my advice and let me solve all of their problems? Didn't my years of education mean anything?

I was convinced I knew everything but confused because I felt like nothing I knew was true. Going into the profession, I had the mistaken idea that the law was black-and-white. That something is either legal or illegal. The answer is right or wrong. That if you find the correct solution you will win the argument, the trial, or the negotiation for your client. I struggled because it was actually all in shades of gray. I would try my best, but other attorneys were not convinced by my rationale. It left me feeling wrong somehow all the time. I was deflated and didn't know how to make sense of it.

In hindsight, I believe what I was really missing at that time was a mentor. No one was there to guide me and show me how to interact, how to present myself in a professional way, and so on. Instead, my bosses were supercritical. One of them said he didn't want to take the time to shape me and train me because I would probably just quit anyway and not work there too long. They paid me peanuts and wondered why I didn't work around the clock. It was clear that I didn't measure up to their standards. They did little to disguise how much they disliked me. A client even called me one day and said the senior partner in my firm told him I was a real bitch. That stung. It was confusing to me that a man who was a retired judge who could have been a terrific role model could behave like a child. And yet, they thought I was the nasty one. How could that be? My reality was to keep showing up for work with a fake smile pasted on my face knowing I was disliked and not going to get any help. Fortunately for me, I lived and worked in a small town and could go home for lunch every day and cry.

Within a few short years, I switched tacks and moved to a new city with better opportunities. After landing a new job in a nontraditional role where I wasn't actually practicing law, the work made me happier for a while. But it lacked any challenges and quickly felt boring. I landed an in-house counsel job and was finally able to thrive for nearly a decade. There, I was able to learn and grow as a professional and I began to develop my own network of contacts.

I found as time went on, I grew frustrated by working for men. In some cases, they had less experience or subject matter expertise, yet they always seemed to be in the managerial role.

One manager said, "Learn to make coffee. Bosses love coffee." He was actually quite proud of this advice and included it on a typed list of other crappy ideas he passed off as wisdom. While I did respect this guy as a lawyer—and I would like to think his advice was metaphorical—it reeked of sexism. I've never seen anyone turn to a man and request something as banal as a cup of coffee. Yet many times in my own legal career I've been asked to serve coffee in a meeting, simply because I was the only woman in the room.

It wasn't until I turned forty that I started to feel like an adult. It was like I began to realize I was not getting younger, and I longed for creative expression. I wanted to do things my way. I needed to live my life on my own terms, and I felt confident I could do it. I had worked with and for men for so long without any wiggle room for being a mom or just a human being. My gut told me I could find room for the needs of my young family and still make money if only I had the freedom to create my own vision. My heart was summoning me to take a chance on myself and try something new. I felt ready to take action and try something totally new. I prepared to leave my reliable, high-paying, in-house counsel job with benefits, to become a freelance writer.

Can you imagine the fear and uncertainty? It truly felt akin to jumping over Niagara Falls and hoping to land on my feet. In my mind those were the only two options. Either I had to stay stuck or make a drastic move and break out of it.

Ultimately, I did freelance writing work and also set up my own law practice so I could take a few clients and still pay the bills. My heart may have been the driving force behind this decision, but my head was still part of the plan. I had to learn to embrace the gray area to move myself out of an impossible bind.

My head was full of questions without answers. Would I be able to make enough money? After all, my family was still relying on me. What would people think and say? I was terrified to tell my parents and risk their judgment of my decision. The voice of doubt in my mind sounds a lot like my parents, who always recommend a conservative approach to life: Live by the book, do the right thing to build security for your family, and always work very hard. But at the end of the day, did I really care what people said? Other attorneys told me I was making a huge financial mistake and that I would only go into debt and never make it on my own. They couldn't have been more wrong.

It was an exercise in faith. And I was a total newbie in the "faith" department. My MO had been to control everything so I didn't have to rely on elements I could not see. After all, I believed myself to be a young, strong, educated woman. What could possibly be beyond my reach? My mother's generation worked hard to advance women's rights so that I could, in fact, do it all. Or at least this is what I grew up thinking and believing.

By this point in my life, I had a husband, two kids, three step-kids, a dog, a mortgage, and a grinding career. I was burned out and increasingly resentful. Doing it all did not leave room for me to breathe, relax, or express myself anywhere in this picture. So with the loving support of my husband behind me, I took the leap.

And you know what? I did land on my feet. It was terrifying and exhilarating, and certainly not easy. There were a few false starts and a million sacrifices to be made. But eventually I grew my own law practice, rented an office, hired staff, and managed to do it while being home after school with my kids. I also had moderate success with my freelance writing work. At the very least, this part of my work opened me up to more creativity and joy. It connected me with a piece of myself that had been missing for decades. Slowly, I began to enjoy practicing law because I loved being my own boss. It meant I could choose who I wanted to work with and set better boundaries to get my own needs met. I had enough flexibility in my days that I could pursue other interests like becoming a yoga teacher and a coach, both of which I am still passionate about. Owning my own business was a major milestone that shaped me into the woman I am today. It was the best decision ever for me.

And yet? The irony is that I recently rejoined the ranks of the corporate world after ten-plus years of being an entrepreneur. I swore for years I would never do this. But never is not a word I would use anymore. Time has changed me in ways that I could not foresee. My kids are older now. Their needs are different and so are mine. Working from home is now an option that never existed for me in the past. More importantly, I now have the confidence of knowing I can make it on my own. I can work for someone else and still maintain a balance between work life and personal life because I've learned to make my own needs a priority. I can embrace the gray area and surrender myself to the process, so long as I maintain a few essential boundaries. There is so much balance and peace in the act of letting go for me now. I understand that I matter. The things I want for myself matter, and that includes trusting my own inner voice over the external pressures of others.

28

ALLEGORY IN FOUR PARTS

Ruth Gould-Goodman

Part I. Allegory: Angel Falling

Angel falls to earth, falls into time and space
Crashes into the boundary of skin
Breath empties
Innocent new eyes
Searching for you, Mother, to recognize an angel

At birth, Mother's heart is supposed to catch me
I wait for her to spread a soft net toward my hurtling descent
But alas, no one is there with loving arms
To catch my fall
Mother does not remember how to catch an angel

For she lives in the land of parking meters and plastic
Since her childhood,
Fear froze her heart.
Doubt shreds the fabric
Of her mother's embrace

I fall into knowing I am alone
I do not matter, nothing matters

Matter does not matter
Struggle to stop my growing terror

No one is present to remember
I Am Daughter of Sun, Moon, and Stars of the Heavens
No one introduces me to the vast oceans, spreading plains
And reaching mountains of Earth
Nor sings lullabies of love to my soul

With no one to reflect my divinity back to me,
I forget that I walk on water,
Hover in timeless spaciousness,
Have wings that fly through all dimensions
With growing silent terror

My eyes search to be remembered
To know I am received and recognized
Long ago, my elders forgot
The ecstasy of each breath
And the song of evolution singing in each body cell.

By the time I am born
Nobody is left who remembers
There is nobody to sing the ancient lullaby of trust and faith
A song born of knowing
All is held by the exquisite intelligence creating everything

Everyone forgot
As they blindly race
Toward a finish line they avoid

Desperate for reflection
I seek validation everywhere
No one is there
Initiated into paralyzing terror
Before there are words
Walls fall away

I learn
What I see with my eyes
Hear from my ears
Feel in my heart and guts
Do not count
I am just a child
I do not know how to do anything right

Invalid as I am I grow
I apply myself to be
What I think others want me to be
I must acquire a PhD to be a human being
Stillness wastes time
Time is Money

I am told that real knowledge comes from books
So, I read and read and read
Become a master at pushing other people's thoughts around
My voice grows inward until I swallow my own words

I become a darkening imploding universe, afraid to speak
I disappear into the walls,
Dissolve so that no one can see me
I deem myself officially invisible

The angel inside begs for reflection
Falling endlessly
Falling into bed with men,
Offering sexuality

"Am I a good lover? Am I lovable? Am I good?"

I begin to eat inconsolably.
Cannot stop eating
My hunger goes out of control.
Seek self in eating
But no matter how much I stuff my stomach,
I never find the answer I desperately seek

Monstrous secrets ooze from every pore
Stare into the mirror for hours
Looking for self in my reflection
See nothing but every tiny flaw

Cannot take my face out of the mirror
Terrified of fat
Fat on my body hisses ugliness
Constantly pinch body fat with meanness,
Expect men to recoil in horror
If they come near enough to touch me
Expect them to shrivel

Believe if a man desired me sexually
I would be OK.

Drown in self-loathing
Mind spits silent self-berating mantras
Blame my body for being so unlovable
One part plots to be rid of the other horrible ugly part

Seek surgical mutilation to get rid of wretched fat
Seek doctors to take a knife to cut the ugly away
On thighs, belly and buttocks

Truth driven into dark subconscious underground space
Truth buried under the facade of "Nice Little Girl"
Who chants the mantra
"That's all right. I know. You are right and I am wrong. Right?"

While inside my heart curdles with shame
Even though a thousand times I decide to go on a diet
Cannot stop shoving food into my mouth

Part II. Meaning

Meaning
Looking for meaning
Find meaning in my longing
In dreams
Roar, cry, laugh
Sit still. Sit empty.

Meaning
Emptiness seeps into the borders
Make soggy any intention to make solid
Try. Try. Trying exhausts

Fleeting images repeat over and over
Start climbing
Fall, fall
Want to arrive but do not know where
Cannot stop falling
Wings clipped.

Voice, arms, legs, hands
Have no power to stop this precipitous descent
Reach for answers in the world
Everyone succumbed
A tsunami of five millennia of forgetfulness crashing

Blind eyes, close ears, shroud heart
All forgot how to
Embrace gently for no reason except to be Love

The dark queen of fear and denial thrives
All falls into dark forgetfulness
Alone
Fragile, paralyzed
Who am I? Where am I?

Desperate to know self
Blindly consume the world
Reject the power of love
Reject the tender embrace of purity
Believe essential innocence
A fairy tale
For children and fools

Fear quickens
War's thunder clangs and flashes
To survive this world of forgetfulness
Learn well the lesson of fear
Soft vulnerable parts armor in hard steel

To survive the harsh desert of self-denial
Become a defensive thorny cactus
Cannot stop stuffing my mouth
Wings clipped, an angel hurtling
Through time and space
Hands, arms, legs and feet flail futilely
Cry through the darkness
To stop this precipitous descent

Each desperate effort pulls soul further from center
Can barely hear the ancient song whispering behind seven doors
"There is nowhere to go. There is nothing to do.
Relax and trust your journey
You are held eternally
By that which created you."

In the darkness of forgetfulness
Only music holds the power
To keep life breathing and imagining itself whole
Forget to forget
Forget to FORGET

Dance my body in an ocean of sound/pulse/rhythm
Will somebody please help?
Will somebody please remember who I am?

Sweat heat body joy
Soar inside music
Body dances

Seduces self to return
Become music
Fly, soar, roar, walk on water
Spirit held by music,
Reclaims its home in my alive dancing body

Dancing, the knowing returns:
"You know you are you
You are you in your unique way.
You know what you need to know.
You are free."

Part III. Ephemeral Premonition of Freedom

Quickly, I lose the thread to my truth
The moment I forget I seek myself outside my center
I twist and darken

The moment I peek out of the dark negative vortex
I created when I was too little to protect myself
I give others the power to give me back to me

Power deflected, siphoned
Vampire
Suck attention to reclaim my own life
Crippled by forgetting
How to claim myself for myself

Terrified to hold space to behold self
Gates slam shut
No one does this to me. I do this to myself
When did I learn to reject being myself?
When did I learn to not be for me

Dreams call incessantly, like a baby crying for its mother
Dreams call me
To love myself as I am
In my dreams
I embrace myself unformed, incomplete, striving, imperfect
An angel falling to find her way back
To center inside the heart of compassion
Music calls the dance from the basement room of dreams
Recalls a beauty—vague and distant
Remember you are the daughter of the sun, the moon, the stars
The vast oceans and spreading plains and mountains of earth
Remember you walk on water and hover in timeless spaciousness
The shroud of forgetfulness slowly drops away
Now know you and I—right here, right now
Only our hearts open to each other will catch our fall
You and I
The infinite web of love immediately touches every star, every heart
Stills our descent into forgetfulness
Choose me as I am
Incomplete, unfinished, and gloriously human
Choose me and remember

Part IV. Voice of My Soul

When I asked, “Where do I come from?” my soul replies:
We come from the perfection of all things
We come from the flame inside the flame
The flame of sublime light that weaves invisibly through everything

We come from the yearning of the heart
The yearning of a man for a woman and a woman for a man

We come from the croaking of frogs
And the smooth sharp nail hidden in the soft fur of the tiger’s paw

We come from the blankness of no thought when there are no more words to fill the space
We come from the water flowing by the gravelly beaches of the riverbank

Where exposed roots of trees reach through earth to connect with water
We come from the silent strength of an oak tree’s branches

Full, heavy, and knurly
Immense weight supported without question

We come from the buzzing of bees intoxicated by the smells of spring flowers
From a mountain meadow after the snows have melted

We come from the unwinding of the nautilus shell, rich glossy mineral being
We come from the hovering of the wave right before it crashes back down to the shore

We come from the mist that rises from the downward cascade of the waterfall,
Catching rainbows in the noonday sun

We come from the eating of a great feast of food fresh from the garden
Apples, oranges, kohlrabi and watercress, scallions and rhubarb,

Spiders and snails and moths and flies
We come from the ropy tail of the great gray elephant with white tusks
and a long intelligent nose swiping flies on its haunches

We come from hesitation and losing our way
And finding our way, again and again
We come from the womb of our mother and the seed of our father
We come from the song of the womb of Creation that sings because it must sing
We come from that song

29

JUST BREATHE

Steph Dodds

My breath has saved my life at least three times that I can remember.
It's simple.
In and out.
Pause and feel.
Hold and release.
Give and receive.
My breath gives me so much information, every moment.
This deep listening offers so much wisdom.
I want to get out of the way and let my breath breathe me. Now that I trust it so much more.
I trust it more than anything, actually.
Now.
I trust my breath to cleanse me and calm me.
I trust my breath with my life.
Literally.
This life-saving and life-giving breath.
Breath is our number one nutrient and we can't live without it for very long.
My breath is saying:
Let me move through you.
Let me cleanse every cell of your body.

Let me love on all of the parts that are hiding, in the dark, painful corners.
My breath is a carrier of healing, of light. And so is yours.

One time my breath saved my life in the ocean, off the beach in Lahaina, Maui. I was swimming out too far from the shore. I didn't mean to. Even though I am a pretty OK swimmer, I like to stay on the safe side and not go out too far. But on this day there were dolphins. Actual dolphins! And I had a snorkel on so I could see them.

Before this I had never seen a dolphin in the wild, especially not swimming next to me. When I put my head underwater I could hear their beautiful squeaking and clicking noises. It sounded otherworldly. There must have been fifty of them in the distance, about four near me. I was in awe as I tried to keep up with them. It was magical. So magical that I hadn't noticed how far out I had drifted. I popped my head out of the water. The shore was far. I had gotten swept up in a riptide. The wind now pushing me further out and further away. I looked toward the dolphins now in the distance, and then I looked back at the shore. I was far. I felt the chill of panic in my whole being. The unbelievable distance silenced the moment.

I thought to myself, "Well … it's swimming or dying. I will need to swim for my life back to shore. No one knows I'm out here. I could sink so easily. I am exhausted. Oh my goodness, no one would know what happened to me. My poor mom." I honestly did not know if I would make it back. I remember thinking, "There are no guarantees in real life either … We don't know if we are going to make it or not. But that makes it life … might as well go for it. I could sink or swim … and then sink. Or I could actually make it."

I could feel my body grow tired and heavy in the waves. It was hard to tell how long I had been swimming. It felt like I had been swimming for hours, but in reality it was probably closer to thirty minutes. I could feel myself start to panic, as if pure anxiety was pulsing in my blood. I didn't have time to panic. I knew if I didn't calm down, I had a 100 percent chance of sinking. Then I remembered my breath. I will use my breath. When I was a yoga instructor, I talked about the breath every day. "OK," I thought, "it's time to breathe." I floated on my back for a bit, catching my breath, doing the backstroke. "It's important to calm down right now," I thought. "I can do this. Just breathe." It took me a while to calm down.

Thank God I had flippers on. I thought I would be fish food for sure if I didn't have these flippers. I started to swim. Backstroke and side stroke, as breaststroke felt like too much. I could feel my arms fatigue, my legs kicking into nothingness, my heart pounding out of my skin. It felt like it was the end of an all-out intense workout, and was time to stop, but I couldn't. My bones wanted some earth to rest on, but there was only the deep blue endless ocean beneath me. Still, I could feel my breath guiding me. There are no guarantees, I thought. I didn't know if this was going to work; there was no one to save me but me. I saw some paddle boarders in the distance saving people who had also gotten swept out in the strong wind and current. But they didn't see me.

I took a little break and gazed at the shore. Still pretty far, was I even getting anywhere? I returned to my mantra, "Well, it's swimming or dying."

Once I got back to the shore, I realized that I had made the choice to swim or die at least thirty times. I was close now, then able to stand, then crawl onto the sand on the beach full of families reorganizing their beach blankets and picnics from all of the sudden wind. They had no idea that it was amazing that I was alive.

I lay on my back, and I laughed and cried at the same time. I was delirious. There was sand everywhere, my hair was matted with salt water and sand. I just lay there, laughing and crying. I was grateful to be alive. I lay there for a while, feeling my heartbeat now pulsing through the sand beneath me, realizing that my breath saved my life. Yoga saved my life. I laughed again and cried again. My mind was wild and tired.

What if I died in the plane crash on the way home after all this swimming? I was in awe of how we have no guarantees in life, all we can do is our best. All we can do is breathe and keep going, that is all we have control over. Years later writing this, I have just as much awe in how we really don't know how things are going to turn out, or if we are going to "make it" or not. I have brought these two nuggets of wisdom forward with me: Just breathe and, well … might as well go for it! Since then, I probably think about the fact that we are spinning on a rock hurtling through space and it is amazing that we are all walking around … a little too often. So much is out of our control, and it can all be gone in a blink. I see my friends use this wisdom without the traumatic experience.

There are so many lessons and nuggets of wisdom from our breath. One of my favorites is that we cannot just breathe out all of the time, or breathe in all of the time. We must have the balance of giving and receiving. A friend of mine says when she is out on a date, she pays attention to how her breath is around that person, as she only wants to be in a relationship with someone who is kind to her nervous system. And her breath will inform her if they are a good choice for her. One of my friends who is a mom, gives her kids the advice of "just breathe" whether they are nervous about trying out for the volleyball team or about surviving military boot camp. Another friend always says that the ability to stay calm is the most powerful and helpful thing you can do in any situation. Another friend of mine lost her twin sister in a tragic accident. Her sister is now her angel, whispering wisdom to her all of the time from the other side. One time she nudged, "Sis, God speaks to you through your breath. If you want to connect to me or to God or to yourself, just breathe."

I trust my breath now. I trust my breath, stay calm, and keep going. That is my decision many times a day. What else am I going to do? I might as well swim toward my dreams, and toward my life, even if I am not sure I will make it. I now pay attention to my breath as if it is the most interesting thing I have ever experienced, as there is wisdom there. My breath informs me if I listen. I notice where I feel my breath in my body. Do I feel it in my chest? I try to breathe down to my toes. I fill up my lower belly with breath as I breathe in, and see my breath moving through my body cleansing me as I breathe out. I see this connection with my breath as a beautiful intimate relationship, with my soul. I feel myself and my soul expand on my breath in, and start new as I empty on the breath out.

Listening and being in tune with our breath keeps us in touch and in communication with our soul. It helps us remember what our humanness has forgotten. Our soul knows that we are the pure essence of love and there is no way to do this whole life thing wrong. None of us are going to make it out of this human experience alive anyhow, so we might as well live. Our souls know that no one else or nothing can hurt us. Our souls know that any problem or perceived problem that we have is just a circumstance for our highest evolution and good. Our soul knows that we are the pure essence of love, and beautiful beyond belief … even though we may not feel sexy or creative or good at anything at all that day. So I keep breathing. I keep swimming because I know it's all worth it.

30

LIVING BETWEEN TWO WORLDS

Sahar Nafal

There is the world of the ego, of identity, of thoughts and emotions. There is the world of the personality that creates our reality.

The world where we want to fight for justice,
demonstrate with judgment for freedom from suffering.

The world that screams for peace and fights for the innocent and the unfairness of the separation of humanity.

There is a dark world that we can easily be entangled in, and be manipulated into believing lies and deception of lower frequencies.

Then, there is the world of highest dimensions. The world
of heart, compassion, and love. The world that unites us as one.

This is the world of the quiet minds, that communicates with the Divine, the highest guidance and the angels above.

The world of evolved human beings, committed to their calling, their purpose, and being of service to humanity.

The world where we meditate and send love, light, and prayers of healing, to all in pain, no matter who they are.

The world where we all agree that right now, compassion for everyone is the only path to peace.

The world of the highest vibration, where love's frequency is expanded, compassion is our religion and oneness is our language.

The world where there is no enemy, no war, no hunger.

That is the world I choose to live in … That is the world that one day I envision every human being will live in.

I see a world without boundaries, only one community on earth. Yes, it is difficult to live between two worlds.

There is much more light in the world that our soul has chosen, there is a world where we thrive and evolve together.

One world, one humanity, one love, one light.

So there won't be space for anything else. I'm choosing to live in that world, to hold that vision … even at times such as these.

ABOUT OUR AUTHORS

TESSA LYNNE ALBURN

Tessa Lynne Alburn is a feminine energy coach, soul connection mentor, and podcast host of *Say YES to Your Soul*. Tessa's mission is to help women have their own divine connection to Source, bring themselves, their ideas, and voices into the world free from traditional systems by breaking through spiritual plateaus and trusting themselves again, so they can experience newfound freedom and magic that fills their hearts and fulfills their dreams. Her passions for learning and adventure have taken her abroad to eight countries, more than twenty islands/territories, and numerous non-ordinary realities. Her favorite outdoor activity is solo SCUBA diving.

YUKIKO AMAYA

Yukiko Amaya is a healer, sacred movement dancer, shamanic practitioner, and priestess of Avalon. She is passionate about restoring our broken relationship with the earth, nature, and all beings. She is the co-creator of Moon Body Temple, a monthly circle for connecting with the flow of the moon and her wisdom. Her healing work, ceremonies, teachings, and sacred immersions come out of her own life experiences, studies with teachers and mentors of various traditions, and guidance from Source. Yukiko is also a writer, working to support restoring our relationship with nature and each other through literature. She lives in the mountains around Shenandoah Valley of Northern Virginia with her husband and their Samoyed puppy and fluffy cat.

Excerpts of her current work in progress can be seen here: literatureofrestoration.org/untitled-yukiko-amaya

Explore more about Yukiko at www.MyGoddessPath.com

SANIKA BHURKE

Sanika Bhurke was born and raised near Mumbai, India, and now writes stories inspired by her immigration experiences in North America. Published here for the first time, Sanika is a proud first-generation Indian Canadian, celebrating diverse cultures and inclusive voices. After living in both Chicago, Illinois, and San Francisco, California, Sanika now resides in Vancouver, British Columbia, with her husband. Her professional life is based in information technology, and before that, she was a Big Four consultant. Sanika finds peace and joy in the mountains, forests, and people of her beautiful new home, British Columbia.

SUSAN BLOCH

Susan Bloch is the author of *Travels with My Grief*, a memoir. Her essays and short fiction have appeared in a variety of publications including *The Forward*, *Entropy*, *The Citron Review, Storgy, Pif Magazine,* and *HuffPost*, as well as receiving a notable mention in *Best American Essays 2017* and placing in the *Travelers' Tales* Solas Awards. www.susanblochwriter.com.

CINDI BUENZLI GERTZ

Cindi Buenzli Gertz helps women awaken the divine feminine within themselves so they can move through midlife and transition to menopause with more peace, clarity, grace, and vibrancy. A Certified Kripalu Yoga Teacher and Relax & Renew Trainer, she shows women how to rest deeply and break through the habits of pushing, pleasing, and perfecting, a struggle she overcame in her own life. In her women's circles, classes, and events, she also draws on her passions for the earth, holistic living, dream insight, the oracle, and the arts—powerful aides in her own healing journey—to design transformational experiences. As creator of the Vibrant Woman Program, Cindi inspires her midlife sisters to design their own joyful journey, come alive again, and thrive with abundance. Subscribe to Cindi's weekly newsletter here: bit.ly/joyful-journey

ANGIE BYAS

Angie Byas is a lawyer and aspiring author who lives in Delaware, Ohio. She describes herself as a creative spirit with a strong desire to support other women in their personal growth. Angie relies on decades of professional experience as the foundation for sharing valuable lessons with others. In this season of life, Angie is focused on serving through her coaching and writing. She and her husband have raised a well-blended family of five and have a German shepherd puppy named Maddy.

STEPH DODDS

Founder of the Emotional Freedom Academy and a DailyOM author, Steph is an emotional freedom techniques (EFT) practitioner and trainer who loves sharing EFT education with the world. She has an international private practice, and offers free tapping videos on her YouTube channel, "Tapping with Steph." Her first book, *How Not to Cry: A Guide to Emotional Freedom for Sensitive People*, is a great beginner's guide for anyone who would like to learn about EFT tapping and upgrade their life experience.

SUSAN DRURY

Susan Drury is a writer, teacher, and transformational healer living in Vancouver, British Columbia. As a result of developing a chronic pain condition some thirty-five years ago, she has devoted herself to uncovering, exploring and working with the deeper mysteries of body, mind, and soul through continued professional training, practice, teaching and writing in a variety of healing modalities, all grounded within a deep meditative spiritual practice. She is the author of *Elevating Your Origins to Love: A Guided Journey of Transformation, Healing and Power* and a living example that it is possible to discover wisdom and love within any circumstance.

MEGAN FLUKE

Megan Fluke is an award-winning environmental advocate and nonprofit leader. As executive director of Green Foothills, her leadership resulted in thousands of protected acres, 260-plus trained environmental justice advocates, and hundreds of thousands of dollars raised for tribes and indigenous groups. She has been recognized by Congress, the California Senate, Santa Clara County, the Santa Clara Valley Open Space Authority, and Greenbelt Alliance. Today Megan serves as a nonprofit consultant and leadership coach, helping organizations and changemakers deepen their impact. She lives in San Jose with her partner and three kids. You can often find her breaking out into song

RUTH GOULD GOODMAN

Ruth is a seventy-seven-year-old white Jewish woman who is on a healing journey her whole life. As with many people who are working on becoming whole, Ruth became an energy healer. She became an acupuncturist and guide into the expressive capacity of our body both vocally, in movement and as an improvisational storyteller. She began to write as another way to enter and shine a light upon her fragmented inner life so it could heal. She healed her body dysmorphia and bulimia through directly entering her pain body to open these creative streams.

AMAN GOHAL, PHD

Aman Gohal works with founders, CEOs and VP leaders across industries helping them become more proactive and increasingly aware of reactive tendencies. Aman is a Master Certified Coach (MCC) and has trained thousands of leaders. She helps leaders develop a conscious and empathetic executive presence through her own Shadow Inquiry™ method and the use of vertical (adult) development. She is passionate about Diversity/Equity/Inclusion and has developed several custom leadership offerings to integrate this work. Aman serves as a faculty member of Georgetown University's Institute for Transformational Leadership Executive Coaching Program where she serves as a codirector and mentor coach (Learning Circle Advisor), teaching the ICF competencies and Faculty of Adult and Human Development curriculum. She also worked as a coach in the Presidential Leadership Scholars Program, the White House Leadership Development program, and the Yale Women's Leadership Program. Aman develops conscious coaches through her own evidence-based Shadow Inquiry™ program, which is accredited by the International Coach Federation.

JENNIFER GOLBUS

Jennifer Golbus is a recovery and mindset coach. She has run two successful communications businesses, but after overcoming the darkness of addiction and rebuilding her life, she stepped into the role of mentor for women ready to make a positive change in their lives. A recovering perfectionist and former self-sabotage expert, Jennifer is committed to helping others identify their blocks, change their inner dialogue and bolster their strengths. She uses a combination of empathy, humor, tough love and proven tactics to help people in recovery, as well as others going through life transitions, find their smiles again. When she's not coaching, you can find her on the beautiful trails of Marin County, California, parenting her two teenagers, or obsessively working to perfect her gluten-free cookie recipe. Reach Jennifer at jennifer@meetmesolutions.com.

JNANA GOWAN

Jnana Gowan, founder of Balance Point Shamanism, is Shamanic Practitioner, Certified Transpersonal Hypnotherapist, and teacher of the shamanic arts. She weaves ritual and sound experiences into her private sessions and community events. Since 1999, she has traversed the healing arts with yoga, Reiki, Peruvian shamanism and other expansive spiritual practices. Immersed in earth-honoring practices for decades, Jnana creates atmospheres of safety and renewal to promote lasting transformational work. To learn more about her, visit her website:
www.balancepointshamanism.com

JANAE HUNDERMAN

Janae Hunderman, a dedicated lifework coach, empowers professionals to uncover their desired contributions and refine their presence. With a background in career and workforce development, she believes that our work doesn't solely define us but serves as a vital expression of identity. Surrounded by Southwest Colorado beauty, Janae explores the trails, nurtures her garden, and channels creativity through electric cello and bass in an all-original band. A perpetual learner, Janae aspires to embody a holistic approach to life, integrating coaching, health and wellness, creative pursuits, and a profound commitment to personal growth into daily life.

HELEN HAYWARD

After growing up in Adelaide, South Australia, Helen worked in higher education in London before training as a psychotherapist there. She taught at La Trobe University when she and her family first arrived in Melbourne, Victoria. Currently, she lives in Hobart, Tasmania, where she mentors other writers, teaches yoga, and looks after a large property. Her third book was *A Slow Childhood: Notes on Thoughtful Parenting*. Helen's fourth book is *Home Work: essays on Love and Housekeeping (2023).*

THEA IBERALL

Thea Iberall has been called "a shimmering bridge between heart and mind." An inductee into the International Educators Hall of Fame, Thea has been published in anthologies and journals including *Blood to Remember: American Poets on the Holocaust*. Her book of contextual poems, *The Sanctuary of Artemis*, traces the roots of patriarchal domination through poetry and essays. She represented Los Angeles at the National Poetry Slam (1998). Thea's ecofeminist novel, *The Swallow and the Nightingale*, is about a four-thousand-year-old secret brought through time by the birds. Thea has a master's degree in writing (USC) and a PhD in computational neuroscience (UMass).

KIM JELLICOE

Kim is a leadership coach, facilitator, and corporate trainer with a passion for bringing out the unique talents and contributions of individuals in a range of settings. Kim's favorite models for coaching and facilitation include the Enneagram or any model that her clients are passionate about pursuing in order to bring about positive change for themselves or their organization. When she isn't coaching clients or exploring facets of the Enneagram, Kim spends her free time supporting her mother in her dementia journey, traveling with her husband, and volunteering for worthy causes in her Northern California hometown.

ARIA JOHNSON

Aria Johnson is a television personality, celebrity voice coach, and keynote speaker. She is best known as the Music Expert on *Beverly Hills Pawn,* the number-one show on Reelz Channel for five seasons, airing in eighty-three countries. With a background as a touring recording artist, Aria founded The Golden Voice, an artist development and vocal coaching firm, committed to teaching young celebrities how to make a positive impact through music.

Her team's efforts have led to multiplatinum record sales, surpassing fifty million album sales and one hundred million views on YouTube, while collaborating with artists from every major label. Aria's work has garnered attention from notable publications including The *LA Times, Star Magazine, Life Magazine, Time Magazine, OK Magazine* and *Woman's Day Magazine*. Aria's mission is to inspire and motivate women to achieve unparalleled success, fueled by self-love, ensuring they reach their highest potential and find profound happiness in the process.

JANET LAWSON

Janet Lawson is a psychotherapist with a background in film and theater. In addition to her bachelor of arts degree in film studies from UC Berkeley, a master's degree in counseling psychology from Dominican University and a master's in library and information science from Indiana University, Janet was a Producing Fellow at the American Film Institute and cofounder of Stichting Quicksilver, a theater company in Rotterdam, the Netherlands. She brings all her skills and experience to work as she continues to develop Autistry Studios, a therapeutic makerspace for autistic teens and adults. She is the mother of an autistic son.

KELLY MASON

Kelly Mason taught creative nonfiction at the Rabbit Hill Writer's Studio. She's written articles and profile pieces for *Rapportage*, a creative nonfiction journal published by the Lancaster Literary Guild. Mason worked as an editor for Big Score Publishing and is currently writing creative content for blog posts and websites, with the occasional fiction story or poem on the side. Mason says she's been telling interesting true stories ever since she learned to speak and is starting to get a little bit better at it.

J. MARK MEADOWS

J. Mark Meadows is a nascent writer and nature photographer in the Pacific Northwest. He relishes long bike rides and hikes fueled by chocolate chip cookies. Raised in Massachusetts and Northern California he was inspired by New England's literary roots, while the expansiveness of life "out West" unleashed his creativity. Son of a Tuskegee, Alabama-born Black father and a White mother from Chico, California, his biracial identity plays a prominent role in how he perceives and navigates the world. These experiences of otherness and belonging inform parenting his two teens and his career as a leadership coach and organization development practitioner.

SAHAR NAFAL

Sahar works with conscious leaders and influencers who desire to play a meaningful role in shifting and healing our planet. Those who perhaps sense that the world is at a turning point and yet they are unsure and unclear about their role on earth. For the past 15 years, she has supported thousands to expand their awareness, consciously evolve, and go deep within to achieve more balance and ease in their lives so they can be an example and away shower in their communities.

Sahar's Soulful Energy Clearing methods, as well her mediumship readings, help her clients heal by soothing their pain, confusion and uncertainty, and releasing whatever is blocking them from finding relief. Sahar's natural gift are passed down from her Palestinian ancestors. Her in-person and virtual circles hold space for healing and expansion for everyone who attends.

Learn more about Sahar’s Soul Guidance Private Mentorship and Readings by visiting Soulfulclearing.com

VANESSA NIXON

As a Traditional Naturopath and author, Vanessa Nixon is passionate about helping women thrive during the spiritual initiation of their menopausal journey. She is adept at attunement to natural health, invigorating dance, and therapeutic movement, and teaching women to see their innate natural beauty. After reimagining her life at age fifty, Vanessa discovered a profound and deeply intuitive process that helped her to embrace her fabulous inner wise woman fearlessly. She now shares these powerful and ancient initiations with women who want to reclaim vibrant good health in their own sacred midlife transit.

ERIN PARTRIDGE, PhD, ATR-BC

Erin Partridge is an artist and board-certified, registered art therapist. She grew up on a ranch in the San Francisco Bay Area, has lived all over California, and spent some time in graduate school in New York. Her clinical experience includes work in community, pediatric, forensic, and geriatric settings and she is published in the areas of art therapy, elder care, and technology. Dr. Partridge's research interests incorporate the lived experience and focus on participatory, ethnographic, and art-based approaches. Her creative process and creative output fluctuate between being intuitive and methodical.

NDIDI RICKERT

Traversing five decades over three continents, this gifted writer and debut memoirist Ndidi Rickert (nee Beckley-Lines) hails from one of the most beautiful countries on the west coast of Africa. Born and raised in Sierra Leone, she schooled in the UK where she obtained her bachelor's degree; she now lives in the San Francisco Bay Area, California, with her husband. Ndidi has twenty-five-plus years of experience in the biopharmaceutical industry. To make sense of her world, she began journaling as a little girl. When not writing, she keeps her love tank full by traveling, visiting family and friends, and appreciating live music. In her spare time, Ndidi mentors STEM children and youth, speaks about accelerating women's rights and policies impacting newborn screening, sickle cell awareness, and is a believer in kindness. Ndidi is a descendant of the Creole people, who were freed slaves and recaptives who resettled in Freetown, Sierra Leone.

LinkedIn Bio: www.linkedin.com/in/ndidi-rickert-she-her-47197371

ANA MERCEDES RIVERA-PAGAN

Ana Rivera-Pagan's stories of life and love are grounded in Brooklyn after World War II. With an anthropologist's eye she remembers a neighborhood peopled with Holocaust survivors, mobsters and a loving extended Puerto Rican family. She's led a diversified life as soldier, medic, personnel manager, and social worker in both the corporate and public sector in service to others. She helped her employers develop value-based cultures that serve their communities and nurture their employees. Looking back, she finds unexpected lessons and surprising ways that growing up a bookie's daughter prepared her for life and leadership.

SUSAN SHLOSS

Susan Shloss is a highly creative being whose media includes poetry, prose, visual art and music. Her mother's passing inspired a flow of poems and prose that are lovingly captured in the piece in this anthology. She is delighted to share her journey with you in hopes that it lends healing and compassion to any losses you may have experienced. With several music and meditation CDs to her name, this is her maiden voyage into publishing her writing.

JOY DYANNE STEARNS

Joy Dyanne Stearns is a grief guide and educator, writer, ceremonialist, modern mystic, wife, mother, and way-shower. Joy has experienced more loss than most with the sudden and tragic death of her child. After her husband died from a heart attack, she then lost her wits and her design career crumbled. She has traveled the globe studying how world cultures handle death and works with monks, indigenous elders, healers, and medicine men. She visited temples, ashrams, and sacred sites around the world only to realize she was the object of her own search. *Beauty from Ashes* is her book in progress.

DAN SWEARINGEN

Dan Swearingen is the parent of an autistic child and a mentor/maker/nonprofit administrator in San Rafael, California. Dan has a master's degree in physics from Cal State Northridge and a master of arts in astronomy from Indiana University. Dan worked for many years in the San Francisco Bay Area as a programmer and manager of programmers before he cofounded Autistry Studios in 2008. A Bay Area native, Dan grew up in San Francisco and moved to Sebastopol as a teenager.

TRUDY TOLIVER

Trudy's professional career was in the management of public sector and nonprofit organizations. She chose places to work that filled her heart and contributed to her community. Trudy worked in public transit, raised funds for conservation groups, and led a world-class farmers market. She let go of all that in mid-2021 to build a home, volunteer, and cultivate her creativity. Building on a long-standing interest in nutrition and fitness, her focus pointed toward the study of wellness as we age. While writing on those topics has yet to gain traction, the learning inspired her deeply.

DAWN AIRHART WITTE

Dawn Airhart Witte is an award-winning humanitarian, author, and speaker, with her proudest title being a mom. Her life's core principle revolves around being the change we wish to see. With more than published books, including the award-winning *Be,* she drives positive transformation. As the founder of the Desire to Inspire Foundation and The Be Line Products, she paves the way for impactful change and personal growth. Dawn also hosts *The Secrets of Being* podcast, exploring profound insights. Her wisdom extends globally, with appearances on podcasts and in publications worldwide, sharing her vision for a better world.

EDITOR AND CURATOR

CYNTHIA GREGORY

Cynthia Gregory is an award-winning writer and author of *Journaling as Sacred Practice: an Act Of Extreme Bravery* (2016), and *What Is Possible From Here* (2021). Cynthia's enigmatic short stories have appeared in a range of publications, including *The Sun*, *Glimmer Train* and *The Briar Cliff Review*, *Santa Barbara Review*, *The Ear*, and *Central PA*. She took second place in the Writer's Digest Fiction Contest and first place in the *Glimmer Train* family matters competition for "Melting At Both Ends," a story about climate change and friendship, and first place in the Mark Twain Short Fiction Prize for her story, "Baby Blood," which explores the complex and mysterious sisterhood of parenting medically frail children.

Her nonfiction food and travel articles have been published in *The Chicago Tribune*, *The Houston Chronicle*, and *Bon Appetit*. She earned her bachelor's degree in journalism from Gonzaga University and her master's degree in literature from Mills College.

Her mission is to expand the body of American literature. She coaches entrepreneurs and community leaders to develop literary legacies in the form of personal histories, works of creative nonfiction, and professional memoirs. Her motto is: "Allow your story to take up space in the world."

Cynthia is a member of the California Writer's Club, Redwood Writers Chapter, the International Association of Women, and the International Coaching Federation. She lives in California's Sonoma Valley with her rescue pups, Winston the Wonder Dog, and the fabulous Mr. Blue.

Find her at:

facebook.com/Cynthia.Gregory.35
linkedin.com/in/gregorycynthia
info.mayacamaspress@gmail.com

ACKNOWLEDGEMENTS

This juicy, soul-deep mosaic of magic and miracles has been one big leap of faith after another. First thanks go to Karen Grace and Nora Joanne Gerber for planning and then inviting me to join them in a silent retreat in Big Sur in early 2023. The genesis of an anthology called *LOVE NOTES From the Soul* formed in a sacred space of stunning natural beauty could hardly be called a coincidence. When one is committed to what potent magic may appear on a silent retreat, generally one does not question what inspired action follows.

The seeds of *LOVE NOTES* found fecund ground in Jessica Hadari's "queen's council" of inspiring entrepreneurial women, many of whom are represented in these pages. There were many allies who encouraged the co-creation of this soul-deep collection where the human spirit shines, who helped edit early versions of the vision, or who shared the call to submit stories for what became the maiden voyage of *LOVE NOTES*. My "accountability buddies" have been an invaluable support in the production of *LOVE NOTES*. Those weekly meetings helped forge the conviction that this book was possible. Huge thanks to my power partners and both formal and informal coaches: Jeanne Sullivan Billeci, Vanessa Nixon, Vivien Monroe, Kathleen Joan, Jo-Anne Weiler, and Sahar Nafal. Respect and propers to my production crew: Nora Joanne Gerber as contributing editor, Crissi Langwell for layout and design, and Mariah Miller for taking the vision of a basic jacket design and giving it the fairy-design godmother makeover it so earnestly deserved. Because it truly does take a village, I would be remiss if I did not thank VA Extraordinaire, Pam Weiser, for her ace organizational skills and grace under pressure. I am forever grateful to and inspired by my extended tribe of clients, authors, editors, teachers, mentors, and assistants.

JOIN OUR LOVE NOTES COMMUNITY

Do you have a story of transformation or resilience or hope to share with the world? Subscribe to the Mayacamas Press mailing list and be the first to know when submissions are open for the next edition of *LOVE NOTES From the Soul.*
hello.lovenotesanthology@gmail.com

LOVE the LOVE NOTES Anthology? Leave a review on Amazon!

www.ingramcontent.com/pod-product-compliance
Lightning Source LLC
Chambersburg PA
CBHW040223170726
48295CB00014B/783

* 9 7 8 1 7 3 7 5 7 4 9 3 4 *